D1536509

The Author and His Doubles

Middle East Literature in Translation

Michael Beard *and* Adnan Haydar
Series Editors

The Author and His Doubles

ESSAYS ON CLASSICAL ARABIC CULTURE

Abdelfattah Kilito

Translated by Michael Cooperson

With a Foreword by Roger Allen

SYU *Syracuse University Press*

L'Auteur et ses doubles Copyright © 1985 by Éditions du Seuil Paris
Translation Copyright © 2001 by Syracuse University Press
Syracuse, New York 13244–5160
All Rights Reserved

First Edition 2001
01 02 03 04 05 06   6 5 4 3 2 1

The paper used in this publication meets the minimum requirements of
American National Standard for Information Sciences—Permanence of
Paper for Printed Library Materials, ANSI Z39.48–1984.∞™

Library of Congress Cataloging-in-Publication Data
Kilito, Abdelfattah, 1945—
[Auteur et ses doubles. English]
The author and his doubles : essays on classical Arabic culture / Abdelfattah Kilito ;
translated by Michael Cooperson with a foreword by Roger Allen.
p. cm.—(Middle East literature in translation)
Includes bibliographical references.
ISBN 0-8156-2936-2 (alk. paper)—ISBN 0-8156-2931-1 (pbk. : alk. paper)
1. Arabic literature—History and criticism. 2. Originality in literature. 3. Imitation in
literature. I. Title. II. Series.
PJ7542.P53 K5513 2001
892.7'09—dc21   2001049782

Manufactured in the United States of America

Our generation suffers from a deep-seated reluctance
to accept anything on the authority of a modern
thinker. Therefore, whenever I want to present a
notion of my own, I attribute it to someone else by
declaring: "It was so-and-so who said so, not I"; and
to ensure I am believed, I say of all my opinions: "It
was so-and-so who invented it, not I." In order to
avoid the unpleasant consequences of having anyone
think that someone as ignorant as myself has the
temerity to offer his own ideas, I let it be supposed
that I have come across them in my studies of Arabic
works. Should what I say displease little minds, I do
not wish to be the one who displeases them. I know
how true scholars suffer at the hands of common
men. Thus it is not my own cause that I plead, but
rather that of the Arabs.

   —Adelard of Bath, twelfth century,
      cited in J. le Goff, *Les Intellectuels au Moyen Age*

Abdelfattah Kilito is a professor in the Department of French at Muhammad V University in Rabat, Morocco, and has published extensively on Arabic literature, writing in both French (most recently, *La langue d'Adam et autres essais* [1995] and Arabic *(Al-Hikaya wa l-ta' wil* [Narrative and interpretation] [1988]). He has been a visiting scholar at the École des Hautes Études en Science Sociales, the Collège de France, and Harvard University. In 1989 he was awarded the Grand Prix du Maroc.

Michael Cooperson teaches at the University of California at Los Angeles, and has written extensively on Arabic literature. His research articles and book reviews have appeared in *Studia Islamica, Muqarnas, Al-Arabiyya, Majallat al-Qahira, Edebiyat,* and the *Harvard Review of Middle Eastern and Islamic Affairs.* His book *Classical Arabic Biography: The Heirs of the Prophets in the Age of al-Ma'mun* was published by Cambridge University Press in 2000.

Contents

Foreword

ROGER ALLEN

The "author" is one who increases (Latin "auctor"), a notion that will be familiar to all who write as a profession. The equivalent terms in Arabic are, first, *katib*, one who engages in the act of writing and thus a term adopted within the context of Arab-Islamic culture to denote a chancery secretary or bureaucrat, and, second, *mu'allif*, one who makes something familiar, one who gathers things together, or composes. Indeed, the term *mu'allif kitab* (book composer) is used to distinguish authors from *mu'allif musiqa*, what we in English call a "composer."

The nature of authorship, the multifarious issues of personal and cultural ownership—questions of identity, of naming, of "authority"—and therefrom the different ways of challenging and subverting such types of ownership and attribution (forgery, plagiarism, and sheer anonymity, the linkages between the oral and written) are the topics of Abdelfattah Kilito's typically brilliant exploration *L'auteur et ses doubles*, which is now made accessible to English readers in this excellent translation by Michael Cooperson. Here Kilito reveals to his readers his unrivaled knowledge of the great compilations of anec-

ix

dotal wisdom in Arabic that were gathered together under a variety of rubrics and of the scholars who sifted and organized them, to which we might add that his references to Western sources evoke a similar pantheon of contemporary critical acumen of French expression— from Arkoun to Zumthor via Barthes, Genette, Lejeune, and Todorov.

Each of the individual chapters takes up a separate issue, and the collection is framed by two segments in which our author, Abdelfattah Kilito, seems to relinquish—if only for a few moments—his scholarly distance in order to involve himself in the narrative. In the Introduction, he returns to childhood in order to become a member of a small group of schoolchildren who ask their teacher after class whether it is necessary to remember the name of the author of a work of fiction (perhaps their real concern was whether such a question would be on the exam). In the conclusion, he—or, at least, his first-person narrator—appears to lose himself in an anecdote about imitation and reintegration; in this case it concerns a lost traveler barking like a dog in order to find his way back to human habitation.

Within the framework of the tales that our author narrates, using all the skills of those forebears who are the primary source for his study, we encounter a host of situations and anecdotes involving ambiguities of attribution and textual ownership. The dog-barking episode comes from *The Book of Animals,* a renowned collection of poetry and anecdote by Arabic literature's greatest polymath, 'Amr ibn Bahr (d. 869) who is universally known by his nickname "al-Jahiz" (the man with boggling eyes). Proverbially ugly, he was ideally suited, so anecdotes cited in Chapter 6 tell us, to serve as a model for the image of the Devil to be placed on a ring as defense against the evil eye. The range of his learning and writings is truly astonishing: from essays on theological controversies to manuals on the training

of singing girls. As is made abundantly clear in his collection of anecdotes, *The Book of Misers*—they being a genuinely peculiar category in
a society in which hospitality and generosity are givens—al-Jahiz also
had a ready sense of humor: if you think the protagonist of this anecdote is mean, he tells his readers, then just wait till you hear this next
story. With good reason Kilito suggests that not merely the sequenc-
ing but also the content of many of the anecdotes in this collection
are the product of al-Jahiz's imagination as well as his artistry. In
other writings al-Jahiz expresses his extreme frustration at the apparently inevitable fate of authors within his own society, most particularly specialists in controversy such as himself: works are either
criticized purely because of the name of their originator or plagiarized. However, there is a way to circumvent this problem: to attribute the work to an earlier writer. Although the procedure may gain
the work some measure of respect, it comes at the heavy cost of
nonattribution to its real author. When later in life al-Jahiz tries to reclaim certain works that, he confesses, were subjected to this mode of
"marketing subterfuge," those very same people who stood poised to
criticize works that he did acknowledge as his own now refuse to believe that he also penned the others. Thus does al-Jahiz find himself
caught in the ironic trap that awaits all narrators who inform their
readers that they are liars.

Within the Arabic literary tradition, poetry is known as *diwan
al-ʿarab* (the register of the Arabs), and Kilito devotes a number of
chapters in his book to the fertile topic of authorship and forgery in
that domain. The study of this poetic tradition is in fact instigated by
the revelation of the Qur'an, itself a "text" with no human author. It
is the processes of compiling, authenticating, and explaining the content of the revelations to the prophet Muhammad that served as the
motivating factor in the young Islamic community's need to find ad-

ditional sources of information and enlightenment on matters not covered by the contents of the sacred text itself. This endeavor included the collection and recording of Hadith, accounts regarding the sayings and activities of the Prophet during his lifetime that were made up of two parts: the details of the event itself and, at the outset, a listing of names through which the transmission process could be checked backward from final recipient to original witness. The phraseology and lexicon of the Qur'an demanded research into linguistic precedents; that quest took early philologists into the desert to record the most famous and readily available corpus of pre-Islamic Arabic, the tradition of poetry that records the life and lore of the nomadic tribes of the peninsula. It was the daunting task of philologists within the Islamic community to develop the necessary critical procedures for the authentication and analysis of these valuable materials from the past that were already the product of an extended period of oral transmission, memorization, and a later process of recording. As Kilito illustrates in several chapters of this book, those procedures shared similar concerns with authentication. At first blush it might seem rather odd to link the obviously serious demands of Hadith scholarship (the topic of Chapter 4) with the demands of poetry and of a pre-Islamic tradition at that. However, it needs to be stressed that, once the poetic corpus was established as *the* linguistic precedent to the Qur'an, the maintenance of its authentic status also became a matter of canonicity. Any attempt to question its historicity constituted an attack on more than the poetry itself; the great Egyptian litterateur and critic Taha Husayn (d. 1973) discovered as much in 1926 when the publication of his famous study of the tradition, *Fi al-shi'r al-jahili* (On pre-Islamic poetry), aroused a furor.

Twentieth-century scholarship in literature and folklore, most especially the work associated with the twin names of Parry and Lord, has now provided us with the means to place the early poetic tradition that the Islamic community recorded into a larger framework of analysis: an oral tradition similar to that of Homer, with an elaborate system of apprenticeship for bards and poets. We now come to realize that the texts of the early poems, as we read them today, are recorded versions of performances, the originals of which stretch back through generations of memory to a point in time when a poet consigned his composition to his *rawi* (bard), discussed in Chapter 5, who frequently became a poet himself; and so the process continued. As contemporary accounts of the training of poets (such as Caton's *Peaks of Yemen I Summon* [1990]) clearly show, apprentice poets gradually acquired repertoires of formulae suitable for types of poem associated with particular occasions. One pre-Islamic poet, 'Antara, wonders at the beginning of his long ode *(mu'allaqah)*, cited in Chapter 1, whether his colleagues have left him any space within which to depict the theme of desert traces. In the study cited above, Taha Husayn questioned the "authenticity" of this poetry as pre-Islamic because he detected post-Islamic elements within it; in the scenario we have just depicted—with bards in the Islamic period carrying on the tradition of each poem from one generation to the next—one might suggest that the absence of such elements would be surprising. What we possess, in other words, with each of these poems is one version of a lengthy performance tradition, each one the consequence of a process of oral transmission and memorization and each one attributed to a poet who may have lived or may not. Khalaf al-Ahmar (d. ca. 797), a compiler of early Arabic poetry, is famous or infamous for the candor with which he acknowledged that he could produce a pre-Islamic poem upon request. In the context of authentication, of course, such a comment may have been cause for concern, but, when the composition and transmission of poetry and the training of its rations into a number of different periods and genres, each one discrete yet linked to the problematics of the book's primary topic.

Let this thoroughly readable translation serve as an introduction in English to the writings of one of the Arab world's most brilliant contemporary literary critics.

Translator's Preface

Abdelfattah Kilito is a professor of literature at the Faculté des lettres at l'Université Mohammed V in Rabat, Morocco, and the author of several studies on classical Arabic literature, including *Al-Adab wa l-gharaba* (Literature and strangeness [1982]); *Al-Hikaya wa l-ta'wil* (Narrative and interpretation [1988]); *Les séances: Recits et codes culturels chez Hamadhani et Hariri* (1983), on the picaresque genre known as the *maqamat; L'Œil et l'aiguille: Essai sur les mille et une nuits* (1992), on the *Thousand and One Nights;* and most recently, *La langue d'Adam et autres essais* (1995), on (among other things) medieval speculations on humankind's first language.

I first came across his *L'Auteur et ses doubles* while preparing for my master's examinations in Arabic language and literature at Harvard University. It proved a delightful respite from, and more insightful than, many a ponderous work of narrowly philological analysis. Professor Kilito's methodology, concisely put, consists in imaginatively reconstructing the cultural assumptions that lie behind a poem or anecdote, and then relentlessly following all these assumptions to their logical, and often contradictory, conclusions. He performs this disconcerting operation on a wide variety of literary texts with a refreshing sense of play and an unostentatious mastery of critical theory.

The French original of the work translated here appeared in a series, *Poétique,* edited by Gerard Genette and Tvetan Todorov, and was presumably intended for the nonspecialist reader. Indeed, the work assumes no previous knowledge of the subject, and can serve as an excellent introduction to the Arabic literary tradition. At the same time, even those readers familiar with the territory, if they allow themselves to feel the child's sense of wonder the book evokes in its first few pages, will find themselves looking at many a well-known text with new eyes. (Readers inspired to explore the tradition further will find an excellent guide in Roger Allen's *Arabic Literary Heritage* [1998]).

Besides the French original, I have referred to 'Abd al-Salam Bin 'Abd al-'Ali's Arabic translation, *Al-Kitaba wa l-tanasukh* (1985), which contains the Arabic originals of the texts cited in French by Kilito. Occasionally I have followed Bin 'Abd al-'Ali in quoting more extensively from the primary texts than Kilito does. (Unless otherwise credited, all translations of Arabic are my own.) Whenever possible, I have quoted from available English translations of works in other languages cited in French by the author. These English translations have been silently incorporated into the references. My very few additions to the author's footnotes appear in brackets.

I extend my thanks to Professor Kilito for his encouragement and advice, and for kindly providing me a copy of the Arabic translation of his book. I also thank Prof. Roger Allen of the University of Pennsylvania for graciously agreeing to write an introduction to the translation. I am also grateful to Dr. Susan Miller of the Center for Middle Eastern Studies at Harvard University for making possible my first meeting with the author; to Prof. William Granara of the Department of Near Eastern Languages at Harvard for facilitating our communications; to Prof. Stefania Pandolfo of the University of

California, Berkeley, for her encouragement; to Prof. Michael Beard of the University of North Dakota for his unfailing support of the project and his perceptive comments on the translation; to Prof. Michael Sells and Wesleyan University Press, for permission to reproduce passages from his *Desert Tracings: Six Classic Arabian Odes* (1989); to Prof. Julie Scott Meisami for publishing a portion of the work in *Edebiyat;* to Annette Wenda, for her expert copyediting; and to Mary Selden Evans of Syracuse University Press, without whose tireless efforts this work would never have appeared before the reader.

Note on Names and Dates

In Arabic names, "Ibn" means "son of" and "Abu" means "father of." An author may be commonly known by his compound name: for example, "Ibn Naqiya," literally "the son of Naqiya." Some authors are known by their first name as well: for example, "Sahl Ibn Harun," meaning "Sahl the son of Harun," which is conventionally abbreviated to "Sahl b. Harun." (The "b." is therefore pronounced "ibn.") The particle "al-," meaning "the," also appears in many names: for example, "al-Jahiz," meaning "the pop-eyed man." "Abu," "Ibn," and "al-" are integral parts of Arabic names and cannot be omitted without causing confusion.

The literary figures who appear in this book represent a range of periods, from the pre-Islamic era (that is, the sixth and early seventh centuries A.D.) to the thirteenth century A.D. Because this is a non-specialist work, Professor Kilito usually confines himself to a brief reference to the century in which a given author lived. More detailed information on all the authors (and genres) mentioned can be found in the *Encyclopedia of Arabic Literature,* edited by Julie Scott Meisami and Paul Starkey (1998) and the *Encyclopedia of Islam, New Edition* (1954–   ).

The Author and His Doubles

Introduction

One day more than twenty years ago, a timid eighth grader, along with two or three of his classmates, approached the French teacher after class to ask a question: when we read a work of fiction, do we have to remember not just the story but the author's name too? The teacher was happy to provide a long explanation, and the student, who had never grasped why there were so many authors, or why stories and school texts always came with an author's name attached, tried his best to understand. He rarely paid attention to authors' names, and even when he did, they made no difference to him. After all, the tops he had spun as a child never bore the names of their makers, just as the stories he heard grown-ups tell bore no signature except the storyteller's inflection, which never varied. Only when he began *reading* stories did he wonder about authors (for it is writing and reading that generate authors and compel us to acknowledge them).

A child believes that stories miraculously tell themselves, needing only a storyteller's voice or a printed page in order to find their way to him or her. One story is as much like another as two currents of water: no matter which spigot you turn, the liquid that pours out is the same. Children might ask where water comes from, but they

1

never ask about the origin or genealogy of a story. As they grow older, they learn to their dismay that every text is systematically provided with a name. For a while, nevertheless, they continue to believe that authors are contingent and interchangeable, docile and transparent conduits for the mysterious force that animates them.[1] The final stage of a child's literary apprenticeship is a melancholy one: the universal Author of their infancy vanishes into the heavens, making way for a host of lesser gods who run wild and give free rein to duplicity and mischief.

Twenty years later, our student related this incident to a group of friends who asked him with a smile what the French teacher's reply had been. The question stopped him in his tracks: he had completely forgotten. He wished he could go back and ask his old teacher once again: why, whenever a book is mentioned, do we want to know the name of its author? No one will read a book without knowing who wrote it, and so we always ask who the author is. If no answer is forthcoming, we speculate; and each of the hypotheses we formulate sets in motion its own interpretation of a work.[2]

The reader who begins with a text and wants to find his way back to the author begins with whatever stylistic devices will point him in the direction of one name or another. Although this procedure works well enough with modern texts, whose styles are as unmistakable as a signature (except in the case of a pastiche), it hardly applies to the texts of classical Arabic culture, where individual style hardly exists.[3] Instead, each genre possesses its own "composition," a set of recurrent features common to a number of works. Given these features, the reader can easily determine the genre to which a given text belongs and move from that text to the consideration of related texts. Yet the reverse, tracing a path from the text back to its author, proves risky if not impossible. Moreover, each of the genres of classical Arabic literature has a number of exemplary practitioners, any one of whose names can be pasted onto an appropriate text of unknown provenance. Anonymity being intolerable, the temptation to attribute the text to one of these exemplary practitioners often proved too strong to resist. Such attributions left classical Arabic texts vulnerable to plagiarism and above all to forgery, since skillful forgers could and did misrepresent their work as that of some past author. We will have frequent occasion to affirm the close link between the notions of authorship and of genre. Authorship is a flimsy notion, whereas genre is a highly specific and determined category, so much so that authors were perhaps nothing but products of their genres.

A speech may be given, or taken away. One can give a speech, take the words out of someone's mouth, or lend one's words to someone else. When X ascribes to himself the speech of Y, it is plagiarism; when X ascribes his own speech to Y, it is forgery. This forgery is the converse of plagiarism. Plagiarism conceals the other behind ourselves, and forgery conceals us behind the other.

The familiarity of narrative form makes us forget the plurality of voices that stories contain. We take for granted the sinuous interweaving of the author's (or the narrator's) voice and the voices of his characters. Yet such has not been the case in other ages and under other skies. In a famous passage in the *Republic,* Plato distinguishes between those parts of the *Iliad* where "the poet himself is the speaker and does not even attempt to suggest to us that anyone but himself is speaking" and those portions where "he delivers a speech as if he were someone else." In the latter case, "shall we not say that [the poet] then assimilates thereby his own diction as far as possible to that of the person whom he announces as about to speak?" [4] Plato objects to this sort of mimesis on the grounds that the poet's constant modulation of his voice to match the personalities of his characters conceals his own identity. This dispersion across multiple incarnations creates the illusion in the reader's mind that the characters are speaking even though the only voice is the poet's and his alone.[5]

Classical Arabic culture, on the other hand, does not permit the sort of narrative mimesis in which the author effaces himself before the speech of imaginary characters. More precisely, classical Arabic literature admits such mimesis only with certain reservations. Authors of fictional narratives in Arabic felt the need to draw attention to the deception inherent in the form, as if their unwary readers were incapable of discovering that they were reading fiction. Most authors who tried their hands at narrative fiction made a point of justifying their enterprise and finding excuses for it. In their introductions, they refer directly to the displacement they have enforced upon their speech, hoping to avoid any misunderstanding, any confusion of shadow and substance.

The question assumes particular interest in view of a seemingly related but actually quite different practice: the attribution of speech not to imaginary characters but to real persons of unquestioned historical existence or to mythical figures no less present and real to the culture than the personalities of history. The resulting "apocryphal" discourse is not the same thing as "fiction" at all. In the case of fictional discourse, various features—conformity to a generic model, the nature of the narrated events, and the status and stature of the characters—reveal it for what it is. Apocryphal discourse, on the other hand, is shorn of any feature that might inspire doubts on the reader's part. Indeed, the apocryphal utterance could never be accepted unless it displayed all the properties of the genuine article. To do his job properly, the forger must take the genuine utterance of a particular author as his model for the fabrication that he will then attribute to the very same author. The result is clearly a pastiche, but so well disguised as to be indistinguishable from the original.

When an author declares his intention of producing a pastiche, we have a form of writing that provokes a reading dominated by the desire to see how well the author of the pastiche has succeeded in suppressing his own voice in favor of his model's. In such cases the reader knows that the text originates not with the author but with another who strives to dissolve into an idiolect not his own. The dice are loaded, but the rules of the game, principally the frank declaration of an intention to be ambiguous, are clearly set out. In the case of forgery, on the other hand, the perpetrator presents the discourse as that of another, severing the umbilical cord that links him to an utterance he has engendered and placed under a name other than his own.

Forgery must also be distinguished from the use of a pseudonym. A pseudonym is not someone else's name but a name one chooses for oneself, and as such is no less arbitrary than one's real name. It does not refer to some person distinct from its user; like a nickname, it refers to precisely the same entity as the real name does. Should it happen to be another person's name as well, it is no longer a pseudonym, and the matter falls once again into the domain of misattribution. In Arabic literature, two or more authors may have the same name, but in such cases some other attribute—for example, an author's place of origin—is usually added to the name by way of clarification.

There is also the case of fictively attributing to a dead author a discourse that treats of a problem he cannot have discussed because the problem was not a matter for discussion during his lifetime. In such cases, certain indications—explicit or implicit—will expose the misattribution. Such indications may take the form of a conditional: were this author alive today, he would say or think such and such. This fictionalization, a sort of prosopopoeia, in many ways resembles a pastiche. The dead sage delivers opinions on matters unknown in his time, opinions constructed on the basis of his personality and system of thought.

One may attribute not only an utterance, but a meaning as well. The Qur'an, for example, was committed to writing at an early period and could hardly serve as a promising object of manipulation by forgers. But even if one could not modify it, or add and subtract passages—that is, use any of the means of misattributing texts to authors—one could still make it say what it never had before. One had merely to postulate a hidden intention behind the text, declaring that the letter of the text was a fiction designed to hide the truth from the unworthy, and that only an elect knows the true meaning of the text and possesses the authority to reveal it to initiates. We know that Western rhetoric was born of a struggle over landed property. Arabic rhetoric is equally the product of a contestation, in this case over the one true meaning of the Qur'an and the ownership of that meaning.[6]

The raw material of language is available to all, but only a few enjoy the capacity to transmute the metal into coin and produce the currency of cultural exchange. In classical Arabic culture, a statement could not become a text simply by conformity to a specific patterning;[7] it had also to originate with or be traceable to a speaker universally accepted as an authority. A text is thus an utterance both authorized and authoritative, solidly moored to an author.[8] An unknown author was hardly to be imagined, and the expression "anonymous text" was practically an oxymoron. Of course, one could express uncertainty about whether a line of poetry belonged to one or another poet. However, the line would still be a text so long as both poets were authoritative names—that is, names whose simple presence transformed utterance into text.

The hierarchy of texts is at the same time a hierarchy of authors. The text par excellence is the Qur'an, which carries the speech of God, the supreme Author. In the second rank comes the Hadith, the words and deeds of the Prophet that provide rules of conduct incumbent upon the believer. A special position—in effect the third rank— is reserved for pre-Islamic poetry, the indispensable source for the codification of Arabic grammar and the understanding of the Qur'an.

These three sets of texts naturally enough gave rise to numerous commentaries. The commentary with the greatest claim to our attention is the fabrication of apocryphal poetry and Hadith. For political and religious reasons, or merely for amusement, one invented utterances and, to ensure their acceptance as texts, attributed them to the Prophet or the pre-Islamic poets. This phenomenon eventually reached such alarming proportions that a safety mechanism had to be installed to curb the expansion of apocrypha and save the canonical texts from counterfeits and questionable manipulations. But how to stop the counterfeiters from plying their shameful trade? The false coins circulating in broad daylight bore every resemblance to the ones struck by the mint, so much so that they could not be told apart: they bore the same tokens and figures, weighed the same, and shone just as brightly. The only difference between the two lay in their point of origin: one was legitimate, the other not.

To prevent inflation and fiscal chaos, it was necessary to purge the market of false coin while preserving the genuine. But in the absence of any intrinsic standard of quality, and in an atmosphere of uncertainty and suspicion, how was this feat to be accomplished? There was only one course to take: trace each coin back to the apparatus that had produced it. Then and only then could one tell whether the coin in question was genuine. One had to start with the holder of the coin, find out where and how he came into possession of it, and work backward along the line of transmission until arriving at last at its point of origin. This act done, one laid one's hands upon the counterfeiters, destroyed their apparatus, and published their names to warn away those people inclined to accept their coins. One could even keep registers containing exhaustively detailed accounts of the names and careers of purveyors of false coin, living and dead, so as to simplify the process of identifying forgeries.

But the forgers proved difficult to suppress. As an inversion of this strategy, or rather as a function of it, another strategy arose to combat it, leaving the two sides to struggle together using nearly equivalent weaponry. The first strategy mobilized massive energies to identify the forgers and publicize their crimes, monitoring their comings and goings and racing to catch them in their lairs. For those people charged with maintaining the purity of the coinage, the battle against fraud came to depend upon an exact knowledge of their opponents' methods. The second and opposing strategy, based on a knowledge of the means of detection at the disposal of the official coiners, exerted every effort to make its handiwork practically impossible to detect. Knowing that theirs was a punishable offense, the counterfeiters concealed their operations and made a carefully guarded secret of the procedures they followed to make a bad coin pass for good. Naturally enough, it often happened that a counterfeiter went over to the enemy, and revealed in his memoirs—sometimes with malice against his erstwhile collaborators—the secrets of his despicable trade.[9]

CHAPTER ONE

Verses and Reverses

The Ruins

One of the most ancient Arabic odes begins with these two questions:

> Have the poets left anywhere
> in need of patching? Or did you,
> after imaginings,
> recognize her abode?[1]

The poet, 'Antara, then evokes the charms of his beloved and describes the ruins of her encampment, which she abandoned before departing with her tribe in search of pasture for their flocks.

Contrary to appearances, 'Antara's two questions are closely linked and perhaps even redundant. Neither permits an answer, as if the answer were either obvious or, on the contrary, impossible to articulate. The poet's question about the encampment follows the query about his predecessors—the poets of yesteryear and long ago, his dead ancestors. The encampments are abandoned and the poets have departed. The melancholy archaeologist 'Antara reconstructs the letter forms of the desert spaces and deciphers the topography of the poetic discourse traced by his predecessors. This sort of poetry inevitably speaks of the old encampments gradually being effaced by the wind and rain.[2] The abandoned campsite that 'Antara recognizes and reconstructs resembles all the encampments ever carved into the soil by departing lovers and absent poets. Much frequented, the path he must follow is already well trodden: he has only to place his feet inside half-seen ancient footprints.

In the first verses of the *Iliad,* Homer invokes the assistance of the Muses. 'Antara for his part invokes the "poets" of the past, the voice of his predecessors, without which no poem may be spoken, or indeed anything said at all. At the beginning of the poem—or rather, at the very beginning of poetry itself—we find a concern for repetition and imitation. The Arabs at the dawn of their history in the sixth century were already hearkening back to an earlier and originary dawn, now lost and effaced (but for its traces), that, for 'Antara, still hovered as a living presence. His own poetry—which we tend to regard today as the first rays of daybreak—already marks the descent into twilight.

By 'Antara's time, the abandoned encampment contained only memories and ruins—ruins that he had to rebuild in order to construct his own dwelling and his own poem. Who could say exactly what his question means? Is his opening line an expression of discouragement, of impatience, of remorse and frustration at having come too late upon the scene? An acknowledgment of debt, a rendering of homage to tradition? Is it an exhortation or a challenge? Or is it a reflection upon what must be said, on the weight of the past and the nature of poetry? Or again he may have intended to lay bare the process itself,[3] as if to say: "If one must begin an ode by describing the ruined campsite, let us obey out of respect for custom; let us follow in the footsteps of the ancients and dutifully conform to their example."

It would seem that the ancient poets did leave something to say. Otherwise 'Antara could not have composed his ode. But what does "leaving" mean? What can the ancients have left to their descendants? And why did they not say everything? Why not exhaust the range of the sayable? Was it kindness or generosity that made them leave to their heirs a lode of discourse to be mined? The verb "to leave" *(laisser/taraka)* is ambiguous. It evokes the image of leftovers, the torches of some bygone feast, freely abandoned by the ancients. Yet it also calls up the image of an oversight on the part of the ancients who, passing alongside some territory of diction, failed to notice it and continued on their way without ever suspecting its existence. In the latter case, it falls to their heirs to lay siege to the territory and conquer it themselves.

In Praise of Repetition

'Antara appears to be thinking not only of himself, but also of every poet who must grapple with a tradition. We may reformulate his inquiry as follows. There is no point is composing verses that do nothing but repeat other verses.[4] But then what would a verse that bore no link to ancient verse even look like? What, indeed, is nonrepetitive speech? Can pure invention, devoid of repetition, give birth to anything but strangeness? Would it not prove in the end to be a deadly mirage: the destruction of speech itself?

Commenting on 'Antara's poem, the eleventh-century critic Ibn Rashiq cites a dictum attributed to the caliph 'Ali: "Were speech not repeated, it would vanish." Speech exists nowhere except in repetition, in the wear and tear of use. To prevent itself from drying up, the spring must flow and squander its waters, spending itself again and again. A word that refuses to be drawn out will languish and dwindle, eventually dying of malnutrition and neglect. Imitation guarantees the life of words, and constitutes the essence of speech. The more one repeats a word, the more it spreads and expands; the same proliferation that kills it brings it back to life. In the beginning was repetition, and no matter how far back into the past we go, we find old words being taken up again and again. In this matter, nothing distinguishes the moderns from the ancients. The heir need not feel dependent upon his predecessors, for he owes them no more than what they owed those people who came before them.[5]

Ironically 'Antara, who thought himself to have appeared after everything had already been said, managed to compose a poem so original—says the critic Ibn Rashiq—that it surpasses the works of the ancients and moderns alike.[6] Even while imitating, 'Antara made his own singular voice resound amid the voices of the ancients. Certainly his voice echoes and reflects theirs, but it has a timbre of its own; it liberates itself by the very gesture of signaling its dependence, and answers its own question—"Have the poets left anywhere in need of patching?"—in the affirmative.

Memory and Oblivion

To better grasp the interplay between imitation and creation, let us return to the abandoned campsite and examine the traces left behind. These traces, according to the pre-Islamic poet Tarafa, resemble a tattooed hand:

> There are traces yet of Khaula in the stony tract
> of Thahmad
> apparent like the tattoo-marks seen on the back of a hand[7]

The poet's gaze follows the lines of the campsite as if they were tattoo marks or lines of writing. Says the pre-Islamic poet Labid:

> And the torrent-beds of Rayyan
> naked tracings
> worn thin, like inscriptions
> carved in flattened stones [8]

A few lines later, still describing the campsite, he repeats the comparisons to writing and tattoo marks:

> The rills and the runlets
> uncovered marks like the script
> of faded scrolls
> restored with pens of reed,
>
> Or tracings of a tattoo woman:
> beneath the indigo powder,
> sifted in spirals,
> the form begins to reappear. [9]

The campsite, the tattoo marks, and the inscription have no sharp or clear-cut design. For this reason the poet is above all else a decipherer of effaced and nearly invisible traces. He must struggle against oblivion, that is, against the detritus that submerges the encampment. Fortunately, the "floods" have swept the earth and exposed what lay concealed. When remembrance removes the veil that covers the old campsites, it revives a faded tattoo mark or worn inscription. The poet's task is to draw new lines over old and write one text atop another. The new writing traces a half-vanished one, and it may so happen that the old, faded letters are copied exactly. Yet the poet faced with the ruins of an inscription must always contribute something of his own to make new encampments rise from the ruins. Oblivion constitutes a prerequisite for the poetic enterprise, and no apprentice poet could afford to neglect it. Here is how the eighth-century poet Abu Nuwas was initiated into the art of forgetting:

> Abu Nuwas asked Khalaf [al-Ahmar] for permission to compose poetry, and Khalaf said: "I refuse to let you make a poem until you memorize a thousand passages of ancient poetry, including chants, odes, and occasional lines." So Abu Nuwas disappeared; and after a good long while, he came back and said, "I've done it."
>
> "Recite them," said Khalaf.
>
> So Abu Nuwas began, and got through the bulk of the verses over a period of several days. Then he asked again for permission to compose poetry. Said Khalaf, "I refuse, unless you forget all one thousand lines as completely as if you had never learned them."
>
> "That's too difficult," said Abu Nuwas. "I've memorized them quite thoroughly!"
>
> "I refuse to let you compose until you forget them," said Khalaf.
>
> So Abu Nuwas disappeared into a monastery and remained in solitude for a period of time until he forgot the lines. He went back to Khalaf and said, "I've forgotten them so thoroughly that it's as if I never memorized anything at all."
>
> Said Khalaf: "Now go compose!" [10]

Drawn to poetry, Abu Nuwas wished to liberate the verses that dwelt within him (or he inside them). But he knew this was not enough: the fulfillment of his desire required him to submit to instruction by a veteran poet. To compose poetry, a poet must seek permission from a higher authority, apprenticing himself to a master who will initiate him into the rituals and secrets of the craft. The first step in the learning process is the memorization of a large number of verses. But the second step—the "forgetting" of what was learned by heart—is disconcerting. A student can train his memory, strengthen his powers of recall, dominate the ebb and flow of his consciousness, and establish mental points of reference—but how can he consciously forget something imprinted in memory? How could one ask or demand that someone forget something—that one erase or cancel out every syllable of a thousand poems? How, moreover, can the teacher who checks to make sure the student has memorized his poems ever check to make sure that he has now forgotten them?[11] Even the student who does not understand the reason for having to wait realizes that he must not begin composing poems as soon as the memorizing is over. By the time he finally obtains permission to compose, "a period of time" will have elapsed during which the thousand lines will disintegrate and become abandoned campsites with nothing to display but a scattering of ruins. Like some natural disaster, oblivion dismembers the structure, rips the stones apart, and scatters the wreckage, turning the thousand poems into a shapeless and indeterminate heap.

Poetic creation reorganizes the wreckage, and in rebuilding, it refashions. Working from the fragments the demolition has left behind, the poet carries out the task of creation: he does away with the old forms and creates new forms out of the chaos of materials scattered before him. In this he resembles "a goldsmith who takes worked silver and gold, melts them down, and refashions them." Every poem has a memory, and the poet must twist and veil the memory so that his auditors can detect only vaguely the thousand and one poems that lie behind the one they hear. The poet, as we have seen, must learn to forget, whereas the auditor for his part must fail to discern the history of the poem that falls upon his ears—the poem being "like an ingot composed of every type of mineral known, as if scooped from a stream fed by various tributaries, or like some wondrous perfume compounded of many scents." [12]

To the similes of the ancient critics we may add another: poetry is the scene of successive incarnations and subtle reincarnations. Every poem has lived before, and not even the most diligent efforts to revive its memory can unearth more than a few scraps of its unique, irreplaceable, and glorious past. But these vestiges sometimes suffice to reveal the past life of the poem, just as surprising and curious as the past life of a word. Just as there are specialists in the life—or more properly, the lives—of words, there are others occupied in organizing, establishing, and compiling the lives of poems. This occupation frequently forms the subject of chapters in Arabic works on poetry and rhetoric, chapters titled *sariqat*, or "plagiarism."

CHAPTER TWO

Adoption

Of all the great composers, Wolfgang Amadeus Mozart was the
least concerned with the composition of *Lieder.* His opus comprises
less than thirty pieces, mostly occasional works . . . some of the
most beautiful of which he gladly disowned and attributed to a
friend.

—W. Oehlmann, *Reclams Liedführer*

Plagiarism

The forms of plagiarism resemble rhetorical figures inasmuch as both
require labels and classifications. In both cases, the further this
process progresses (or regresses), the more complex the taxonomy
becomes and the more diversified the labels. Any critic interested in
plagiarism finds the terrain already bristling with signposts. In order
to advance with any facility, he must rearrange the markers—if only
to avoid being accused of plagiarism. Not even by speaking of plagiarism can one avoid it altogether.

The Arab critics do not necessarily condemn plagiarism. Appro-
priating the work of others without crediting them certainly merits a
certain disapproval, but the question remains whether it is desirable

or even possible to do without the discourse of others. Ibn Rashiq has no hesitation regarding this matter: "No poet can claim immunity from plagiarism."[1] The closure of a text is unthinkable: every line of every poem contains the echo of other lines and other poems, and the composition of verse can only entail the plagiarism of other verses.

In this connection we may note the prescriptive nature of classical Arabic poetical criticism, which takes older experiments in composition as the basis for the strict rules it imposes on the craft. Even exceptions and violations lose their transgressiveness with the passage of time and eventually become the basis for new and equally rigid rules. The poet is called upon to duplicate a fixed model, and in his attempts to follow the directions on the label,[2] he cannot avoid plagiarizing from the model.

The Arabic word corresponding to "plagiarism," *sariqat*, must be understood in a very broad sense.[3] Whenever we can discern a relationship between a text and one or more older texts, we are dealing with a plagiarism. Citation is a form of plagiarism, and many critics discuss it in their chapters on *sariqat* or in an appendix to that chapter.[4] Of the five types of *sariqat*, the first two refer to the nature of the source text: *iqtibas* is the use of verses from the Qur'an or the Hadith of the Prophet, and *tadmin* is the use of one or more lines of poetry. The second two types refer to a transposition from one register to another: *hall* is the rewriting of poetry as prose, and *'aqd* the reverse.[5] The last type is *talmih*, allusion to a well-known event, personality, or story.

We can reduce all the phenomena studied as *sariqat* to the category of allusion. Since no poet can avoid plagiarizing, every line of poetry is in principle allusive. A poet may combine several lines into one of his own, transfer a motif from one genre to another (from love poetry, for example, to praise poetry), rewrite a line in a different meter, collapse a line into a half line, spell out a hidden meaning, or redeem a line of doggerel with a finer elocution. Plagiarism, in sum, occurs whenever a poet borrows an idea *(ma'na)* and gives it new expression *(lafz)*.[6]

The Fathering of Meaning

The Arabic critics distinguish three types of poetic ideas. The first is the anonymous, "orphaned" idea: one that has no progenitor or whose progenitor is unknown. These commonplaces fall within everyone's reach; they include the comparison of a brave man to a lion and a generous man to a rain cloud. That such similes were considered universal exemplifies the naturalization of culture-bound conceptions.[7] We may admit that all cultures praise courage and generosity, and even that the comparison of a brave man to a lion exists in many cultures,[8] but the comparison of a generous man to a cloud makes sense only in Arab (and, perhaps, in similarly constituted) cultures, where the appearance of rain is an occasion for rejoicing. The reader who has never known that culture firsthand might well have difficulty conceiving how ardently the Arab poet hopes to see a rain cloud shedding torrents upon the encampments of the beloved or the grave of a dead companion.

Orphaned ideas lose their anonymity when a poet adopts (and adapts) them, clothes them in new dress, and pronounces himself their progenitor. Likening a generous man to a cloud is familiar; saying that the clouds are shamed by his generosity constitutes a renewal and a reappropriation of the original meaning.[9] This second category of ideas is called invented or procreated *(muwallad)*. Invention *(iktira', "making pliable")* is compared to a sexual act: the poet is a stallion *(fahl)* who opens a path [10] and, in a word, deflowers the idea.[11]

Other poets, for their part, will fall upon the newly fathered idea and attempt to appropriate or imitate it. Imitation counts as the "fathering" of a new idea as well, and the imitation is compared to the "mother idea" and judged against it. The daughter idea will be fertilized in its turn and give rise to verses of its own, and an entire progeny will come into being. Imitation is a competition between an original and its derivatives, the latter striving to triumph over the former. When the imitator succeeds, the result becomes associated with his name, although he did not invent the idea to begin with.[12] Nevertheless, his ascendancy is short-lived, with various competitors threatening to wrest away the palm of victory. Ideas thus form the stake in a battle where victory has all too short a lease.

If an idea submits to continuous acts of fathering, it does so because it suffers from a deficiency or incompleteness. It demands that poets make up the lack and carry the meaning to a higher state of perfection. In some cases, however, imitation proves impossible, as when an idea—now of the third type—resists any further fertilization, that is, when it proves sterile.[13] This attribute is not at all pejorative; rather, the reverse is true. A sterile idea in its perfection renders all imitators impotent. Anyone who makes the attempt comes away disappointed, for the idea is "a splendid tree that bears no fruit."[14]

The Monopolist

The poet Jamil, of the tribe of 'Udhra, included in one of his poems the following verse:

> Whenever people march—behold! they march behind us
> And if we make a sign to them, they halt.

One day as Jamil was reciting this line, al-Farazdaq, the poet of Mudar, accosted him. "When were the sons of 'Udhra ever kings? Kingship is of Mudar, and I am their poet." [15]

In other words, al-Farazdaq was claiming that the verse was his and not Jamil's! The latter credited his tribe with a virtue it did not deserve and so *should not have spoken* the line. Al-Farazdaq, on the other hand, *could have spoken* the line, because he represents a tribe with a real claim to glory. The line befits him, which suffices to make him its author.

The line itself belongs to the genre of "vaunting poetry," the register in which al-Farazdaq particularly excelled: his lampooning of hostile tribes and his eloquent praise of his own were well known. Certainly he was not the only poet to compose in this genre, but he excelled in it so conspicuously that when his name is mentioned it is always his vaunts that come to mind. As for Jamil, he hardly composed a line in any genre but the erotic. Most of his odes are devoted to his love for a woman—always the same Buthayna. We do not expect him to compose a verse of vaunting poetry: it is not his "way" *(tariqa)*, nor does it fit the image that has been constructed for him. The line cited here sullies the purity of that image; it dangles like a useless and awkward appendage from the corpus of his poetry; it lurks like a poor, eccentric relative, unneeded because unconnected to the rest of Jamil's oeuvre, a mismatched pearl in the necklace. Claimed by al-Farazdaq, however, the line finds itself on familiar territory, among relatives and friends. Al-Farazdaq may therefore claim it without scruple or hesitation.

It appears that Jamil ceded him the line willingly, "dismissing him and it both"; [16] he was, after all, returning al-Farazdaq's property. Had Jamil misattributed it to al-Farazdaq, no one would have taken offense. Had al-Farazdaq credited it to Jamil, no one would have believed him. Indeed, had the line simply wandered, lost and anonymous, it would doubtless have been attributed to al-Farazdaq. In this instance of "plagiarism," the plagiarist, paradoxically, is Jamil, because he imitated al-Farazdaq's manner; "his" line smacks of mimicry. True, Jamil evinces skill by composing a line in an unfamiliar genre, but it is a contrived sort of skill, a parroting that may provoke astonishment but never applause.

What would have happened had al-Farazdaq seized a line of erotic poetry belonging to Jamil? The claim would have triggered the most violent objections, as Jamil had already proved himself superior in the composition of love lyrics whereas al-Farazdaq's erotic verses are simply mediocre.

In his chosen register, al-Farazdaq was a remorseless monopolist. Should lines of vaunting charm him, he would ask their composer to forbear reciting them in his own name. Should the composer resist, al-Farazdaq would resort to blackmail and intimidation. Such threats were inevitably effective, because the victims of his lampoons never recovered.[17] All the same, the lines he acquired—with or without the consent of their owners—would remain associated with their original composer. Everyone recognized that the lines befit al-Farazdaq, but everyone also knew the names of their real composers. The lines became bisected, torn apart, endowed with two heads, each looking a different way. When recited, they would be attributed both to the poet who had spoken them without being worthy of them and to the poet who was worthy of them without having spoken them.

Similar is the case of poets who "selected certain of their verses as gifts for their colleagues." One might attribute them to their composer, but he had refused to adopt them in the true sense of the word, because he had composed them with the intention of giving them up.

Such cases resemble forgery, as when A puts himself in the place of B
and behaves as if he were B. Ibn Rashiq comments on "gift giving" as
follows: "A poet may ask for a gift of one, two, three, or even more
lines if they correspond to his way *(tariqa)*. This is not counted a
fault, since the poet is capable of making similar verses for himself;
but it is only permitted to the sharpest and most renowned of
poets." [18] In other words, a great poet may "plagiarize" verses in the
genre he has mastered; all roads will lead the lines back to him.

Abu Yasin

There once was a man named Abu Yasin who could perform mathe-
matical calculations faster than anyone else. Unfortunately, he applied himself too intensely to a problem and went mad. In his
delirium, he claimed that he would become a king, and that he could
foresee battles and other major events that would one day come to
pass. Among his acquaintances was the poet Abu Nuwas, who—
doubtless to amuse himself—attributed to Abu Yasin poems appropriate to his ravings. Abu Yasin would learn these poems by heart and
claim them as his own. [19] Everyone knew better, but Abu Yasin remained convinced that the verses he recited were his own. He was
not so far from the truth, as he was the only one who could adopt
poems so eminently suited to him alone. True, Abu Nuwas had composed them, but because he did not claim prophecy for himself, he
could not claim responsibility for the content of the poems; he could
only step into Abu Yasin's shoes and live out, as a game, his obses-
sions. In the meantime, Abu Yasin, unable to maintain a distance
from the images that filled his disordered imagination, actually believed himself a king, a seer, and a poet.

CHAPTER THREE

The Polyandrous Ode

The Errant Tailor

Panegyric is the site of a contract, spoken or unspoken, between a poet and a prince. In return for money, the poet offers praise. His contract comes into effect the moment the prince agrees to hear him. If the prince closes his door and refuses to receive the poet, the prince incurs no obligation. On the other hand, he may take the initiative by giving money to a poet who then composes a panegyric to demonstrate his gratitude. Relations between the two parties are often strained, and one or the other frequently fails to uphold his end of the bargain. The prince may skimp on the poet's prize, dismiss him outright should he judge the verses mediocre, or make promises to him he later "forgets." Do not, however, hasten to pity the poet for his dependence. He was not born yesterday either, and he has more than one trick up his sleeve. He can satirize the prince he has praised, and drag him through the mud after having compared him to the sun. Yet this is a run-of-the-mill sort of revenge. More tellingly, he can resort to a perfidious, perverse, and outlandish trick—one that I shall attempt to study here—namely, using the same ode to praise several different princes.[1]

24

When a prince pays for a panegyric, he becomes its owner. More exactly, he seizes sole control of it, which holds true even if he treats the poet ungratefully. The ode has only to be addressed to the prince to become attached to his person exclusively and forever. He appropriates the poem simply because it depicts his qualities and his virtues, in the same way he would appropriate a portrait of himself. It would never occur to anyone else to claim the portrait, or at least not the image it contains.[2] A person who sits for a portrait always has the power to defeat any rival claimants to the image simply by placing them before the painting. Unless they happen to be exact doubles of the sitter (unlikely indeed, for one never meets doppelgängers in the street, only in books), they will be forced to admit that the portrait they claim does not reflect their own image as a mirror would.[3] Moreover, the margin of a portrait usually bears, besides the name of the painter, the name of the subject as well. If, for one reason or another, the name of the sitter is unknown, the portrait will still represent one and only one individual.

The same holds, it would seem, for the panegyric. Collections of poetry and literary anthologies mention the name of the prince to whom the ode was dedicated in the same breath as that of the poet himself. The ode, furthermore, often contains evidence of the prince's identity: his name, allusions to his accession, battles won, and feats discharged. One can be certain that a specific prince is meant, even when one happens not to know exactly who he is.

But it is the matter of the "one prince" that points up an essential difference between the panegyric and the portrait. The portrait is inseparable from the canvas, and the sitter remains familiar even in copies made of the original. This original, moreover, remains the same no matter how often it is reproduced. The panegyric, on the other hand, stands free of voice and of writing. The first recitation or first written record of it has no privilege over the ones that follow it, a state of affairs clearly different from that which obtains in the case of a portrait. One can even say that the panegyric is independent to a great extent of the prince to whom it is addressed, because—as in other traditional genres—it describes the prince by reference not to individual traits, but to typical ones. The poet praises not such and such a caliph, but an ideal caliph; not the minister so-and-so, but an ideal minister. How is one to tell, then, whether a given panegyric was composed for X or for Y? Only common knowledge can decide one way or the other. The link between prince and poem is contingent, and by virtue of this contingency, a game of hide-and-seek comes into being.

The critics of Arabic poetry set up rigid barriers among the various types of persons a poet might praise, including kings, ministers, generals, scribes, judges, and commoners.[4] To praise a minister in the terms used to praise a king or a general would be a grave mistake. It is inadmissable to praise a king for setting a well-laden table: this trait better befits one of his chamberlains. It would be equally insulting to say of him that he keeps his word, a compliment meaningful only if applied to a commoner.[5] To each type corresponds an appropriate discourse, a series of attributes proper to him and to him alone.

It is at this juncture that we find the comparison of discourse to clothing.[6] The ninth-century poet Abu Tammam gave the following piece of advice to one of his students: "Be like the tailor who cuts his cloth to size."[7] Here again, the reference is not to individual measurements: the suit must be a collective one, into which all the bodies who belong to the same social corporation must fit. Yet Abu Tammam's comparison seems to fail on one count. When a suit is fitted to a customer, it becomes his property, matching his build and adapting itself to his proportions. But if many people share his build and his proportions, would they not be tempted to claim his suit for their own?

This situation will arise only if the tailor accepts payment for the same suit from several different customers. As he proceeds with his work, the customers will try on the suit (one by one, of course, to prevent the discovery of the trick). Then comes the moment of truth, the day when the tailor must deliver the goods. What does he do? He packs up and goes off to ply his sordid trade in another town. Of course, he takes the suit with him. There is no one to whom he could leave it, because it fits all his customers: why should he favor one of them at the expense of another? The simplest solution is to remove it, thus avoiding a dispute among the jealous customers. Moreover, he can use the suit as bait the next time around. Of course, a difficulty may arise at his new place of business if a customer wants to buy the completed suit as is. To forestall this possibility, the tailor must take the suit apart, unstitch it, and return it to its original state of plain fabric. One may easily imagine him repeating this operation, once again selling the unfinished suit to several individuals, and then, when the suit is ready to wear, taking to his heels.

In parallel fashion, the poet has the ability to use the same poem again and again to praise successive princes. All he has to do is, while on the road, perform minor alterations to the fabric of his poem and remove such details (a name, for example) that give away the connection to the prince whom he has decided to strip of the suit. He can even avoid mentioning any details that might evoke a particular prince in the first place and thus save himself the trouble of having to modify the poem later. The panegyric will then fit everyone, and no one. In the most extreme case, the poet need never compose more than one poem in his life.

This possibility is not simply theoretical; classical poets actually did exploit it. Abu Tammam, whom I have just cited, and above all his disciple al-Buhturi, leave themselves open to criticism on precisely this count. The recycling of a poem is a sort of self-plagiarism, an entirely legitimate practice (for all that it may reflect a lack of inventiveness) that constitutes a deception only when the poet disguises it by telling the prince that the panegyric addressed to him is a virgin poem unsullied by other hands.[8]

Clearly the trick cannot succeed when the poet attaches himself to a court. Unless he puts himself to the trouble of composing a new panegyric for each occasion, he will receive no reward. On the other hand, the errant poet, who wanders the world pandering as he goes, coming from afar and departing again, is subject to no authority. He is free to hawk his wares in perfect confidence. Yet he must run a little faster every time as he moves from one court to another. Otherwise his poem will precede him and he will find himself unable to recycle it. As an old metaphor would have it, the poem is a runaway camel on an erratic and unpredictable course: one cannot tell where it will end up nor who will care for it. The successful panegyric can work only once, for it outraces the poet, finding its way to far-flung climes and peopling the memories of men. Trapped by success and made a virtuous man despite himself, the poet loses his hold over his ode, which becomes the undisputed property of the prince.

The Poet's Daughters

Self-plagiarism—that is, the recycling of one's own poem—creates considerable problems for poet, prince, and audience alike. How, for instance, would an anthologist label a panegyric offered to several princes? Should he list in order all the princes who believed they bought the poem when in fact they had only borrowed it? Or should he mention only the first prince to whom the poem was dedicated, on the grounds that having come first gives him a certain privilege over the others? As for the poet, he is condemned to dodging all the princes he has ever praised on his various stops. Eventually he will acquire a reputation for being a fraud, and no one will accept his praises. Regarded everywhere with suspicion, he can never redeem his honor: any prince he addresses will turn away from him in contempt. Even when he offers his assurances that the poem has never been used before, doubts will persist, regarding the future as much as the past. Even a prince willing to believe that the ode is a virgin poem will have difficulty believing that it will not soon be taken from him and offered to someone else.

Most frustrated of all are the princes who have each paid the bill for their panegyric only to discover that the poet has hoodwinked them all. For some period of time, each imagined that the suit had been tailored especially for him. Now he finds that he is wearing a secondhand suit and living in an unbearable sort of promiscuity. Suddenly the suit seems shabby and redolent of all its former owners. A prince has himself praised to enhance his reputation, to keep his name on everyone's lips and make his merits known to the world. But now, instead of appearing to be a superman, he must resign himself to being a dupe and come to terms with his fellow victims. He believed the ode's hyperbolic imagery to apply uniquely and exclusively to him, but now it appears repetitive and common. He is the others, and the others are he.

Ibn Rashiq very sensibly recommends that the poet reuse an ode only when the addressee refuses to pay for it.[9] In this case, a new contract comes into effect, but the memory of the first contract threatens to cast a pall over the reception of the ode. It is forever associated with two princes, the one who paid for it and the one who did not.

One can also imagine another sort of confidence trick, this time played by the prince: he could refuse outright to reward the poets who sing his praises. Such a policy is hardly practical, however, because the poets would then refuse to have anything to do with him. Eventually one would brand him with a poisonous satire and stigmatize him forever. Indeed, satire is the last card the poet can play when the prince tries to shirk his responsibilities. Certainly the poet derives no material advantage from it (he remains as poor as ever, and in addition has to seek refuge with another prince), but he satisfies his desire for vengeance. Most important, he acquires the reputation of a man who never forgives—a reputation that will protect him from anyone tempted to deny him his due. The ode that goes unpaid for may never find any takers, especially when the news gets around that the poet's "daughter" was already married off once—and without a dowry at that.

Reproached for prostituting his odes, a certain poet protested: "They are my daughters, and I marry them off to whomever I want!" [10] I admit to not having completely understood the analogy. When he gives his "daughter" in "marriage," a poet collects a "dowry"; to collect more than one dowry, he must give his daughter to more than one prince. As polyandry is impermissible, the multiple marriages must remain a secret; the husbands must suspect nothing. Promising the daughter's hand is easy enough, but it is impossible to hand her over to more than one husband—at least, not at the same time, although the bride could move from one husband to another in succession. This subterfuge could take place only if each of the husbands consented to let her go, which is where the analogy rings false. In reality, a father or guardian can give away a daughter only once. As soon as he settles on one of the suitors, he cannot go back and change his mind. Now none of the princes would consent to let the poem he has paid for go off with someone else, and so the poet can take his poem away only by surprise, sneaking off with it so he can offer it to another prince and play the same trick again. The analogy works only if the poet respects the terms of his original contract with the prince in every regard. But one can still imagine the sordid escapades of a father who travels the world and gives away his daughter at every stop, collecting a dowry, and then fleeing with her into new adventures.

Self-Plagiarism and Forgery

Could self-plagiarism of the sort just described function in the case of genres besides the panegyric? At first glance, satires *(hija')*, love poems *(ghazal,)* vaunts *(fakhr,)* and elegies *(ritha')* all lend themselves to recycling. A poet can attack different enemies with the same satire, praise the beauties of several women with the same love poem, sing his own praises again and again with the same vaunting poem, and mourn numerous dead men with the same elegy. Rather than systematically considering all the traditional genres from this standpoint, I will simply claim that self-plagiarism constitutes a deception only when the poet composes with a material reward in view. For example, self-praise cannot possibly give rise to fraud because the poet, apart from whether his audience is familiar with the poem, has nothing to gain by claiming that his work is now being recited for the first time. In any case, the vaunt has no part in a contractual agreement like the one that governs the panegyric. In the case of the vaunt, the poet is not seeking to exchange his verses for money but rather to show off his claims to glory and prove his mastery of the art of self-praise. The same holds true for erotic poetry, which in the final analysis is addressed not to the beloved, but to lovers of poetry. One too often forgets that the poet pays court to his fellow experts more than to anyone else.

As for satire, one can hardly claim that the poet breaks a contract by using a poem again. Unlike the panegyric, the satire is composed not with monetary gain in mind, but rather in the interest of moral and emotional satisfaction. Redeployment can only weaken a satire. Directed at several objects, it loses the edge that derives precisely from its applicability to a specific individual. Imagine that a poet is paid by one party to satirize another. The poet could later fob off the same poem to another patron making the same request, but only if the success of the poem the first time around has not made it indelibly bound to its original victim.

What of the elegy? The elegy praises the merits of one deceased, and differs from the panegyric only in one formal property: the use of the past instead of the present tense. Rather than "He is . . ." or "You are. . . ," we have "He was . . ." or "You were. . ."[11] Besides this idiosyncracy, the genre upholds all the rules that govern the panegyric, first among them the appropriateness of the praise to the status of the person addressed. With whom does the poet establish his contract? Not with the deceased, who is no longer there to reward him (unless the poet is composing in loyalty to the memory of a prince who treated him well), but with a relative. The poet may well reuse his elegy, mourning all the dead men who happen along without ever bothering to compose a new poem. One limitation, however, does exist. Although the poet can knock on the palace gates at any time to offer a panegyric, he cannot always be at the right place at the right time in cases of death. For the itinerant poet, occasions for pronouncing funeral elegies come rarely and unexpectedly; for this reason, Arabic poetry preserves fewer elegies than panegyrics.

We have seen the panegyric attach itself to several persons when it is reused. We have also seen that cheating is possible because the genre describes qualities appropriate to all the representatives of a given social category. The polyandrous ode resembles texts whose authorship is uncertain but whose subject and style call to mind the names of several authors. That is, one can attribute all such works indifferently to A, B, or C. What applies to patrons applies equally well to authors. Both are placed in watertight categories, social ones in the case of patrons and literary ones in the case of authors.

Like the self-plagiarist who reuses his poems, the forger works with categories and, within each category, with a fairly large number of individuals. When the forger seeks to make a false attribution of a text to a dead author, he confronts an embarrassment of riches, because each genre has several authors to represent it. It makes little difference whether the text is listed under the name of A or of B, so long as both are canonical representatives of the genre to which the text belongs. Nevertheless, the forger must take the same precautions the self-plagiarist does. That is, he must avoid inappropriate attributions. He must not attribute to A a text worthy only of B; he cannot, for example, attribute heretical pronouncements to a champion of orthodoxy.

One significant difference nevertheless exists between the self-plagiarist and the forger. The former will sooner or later find himself unmasked; the exposure of his confidence trick is only a matter of time. The latter, however, if a skillful master of the rules of forgery, can disguise his handiwork so carefully that it becomes impossible to spot. He will be revealed as a forger only if he should one day decide to make a spontaneous confession of his crimes.

CHAPTER FOUR

The Paths of the Prophetic Hadith

In its implications, the distortion of a text resembles a murder. The difficulty is not in perpetrating the deed, but in getting rid of its traces. We might well lend the word "Entstellung [distortion]" the double meaning to which it has a claim but of which today it makes no use. It should mean not only "to change the appearance of something" but also "to put something in another place, to displace." Accordingly, in many instances of textual distortion, we may nevertheless count upon finding what has been suppressed and disavowed hidden away somewhere else, though changed and torn from its context. Only it will not always be easy to recognize it.

—Sigmund Freud, "Moses and Monotheism," in *The Standard Edition of the Psychological Works of Sigmund Freud*

An Outraged Father

One day a child came home from Qur'an school in tears. His father asked him what happened. When the child replied that the teacher had struck him, the father flew into a rage against the teacher and against all teachers past, present, and future. "By God," he said, "I'll show them!" How? To condemn them to everlasting shame, he had only to cite the following pronouncement: "Of all men, your children's teachers are the worst!"

This declaration can hardly go unchallenged. Not all schoolteachers are wicked, and the child in this case may have deserved a beating. Moreover, the father had spoken in the heat of anger and would express himself more fairly once his anger had subsided. At any rate, abuse cannot suffice to make all schoolteachers villains. But the father was careful to introduce his outburst with an imposing list of authorities. Instead of presenting the curse as his own, he presented it as spoken by the Prophet, as follows: "'Ikrima informed me, on the authority of Ibn 'Abbas, that the Prophet—may God bless and save him—said: 'Of all men, your children's teachers are the worst.'" The outraged father first cites his source for the Prophet's statement, namely, 'Ikrima, and then 'Ikrima's own source, Ibn 'Abbas. In this way he supplies the list of authorities that guarantees the reliability of the transmission of the Prophet's words. Taken together, the text constitutes a Hadith, that is, a prophetic dictum—in this case, as it happens, an apocryphal one.[1]

The Hunt for Knowledge

The Muslim worldview considers the period of the Revelation to be an originary and privileged time. For twenty years, God spoke to the believers and indicated, through the voice of his Prophet, what men and women should or should not do. Whenever a need arose, God interfered in human affairs, settling differences of opinion and resolving the thorniest problems. Upon the death of the Prophet, no intermediary was left, and Heaven fell silent once and for all. In vain did the believers raise their eyes and search the blue immensity of sky, but no sign was forthcoming. A breach had opened never to be closed, and struggles for power began that were never to end.

As the past grew ever more distant, the believers' longing for it grew, and nostalgia weighed ever heavier on their hearts. A sin had been committed, as serious as that of Adam. The only way to atone for it was to renew the ties to those believers who had lived at the time of the Revelation. How could this feat be accomplished? By scrupulous adherence to the precepts of the Qur'an, the repository of the Word of God. But the Divine Book is not always easy to understand: it contains ambiguities (such as, is the expression "the hand of God" to be taken literally or metaphorically?), apparently conflicting assertions (for instance, man's deeds are predestined, but he possesses free will), and eschatological references of a controversial nature (for example, will the faithful enjoy the "sight" of God in the Hereafter?).

The Prophet was no longer present to clarify these subtleties. However, during the time of his mission, he had acted and spoken, addressed individuals and groups, adjudicated disputes, and answered questions posed by people who visited him. Nothing could be simpler than to rely upon his words to resolve the difficulties of the Qur'an and confront the problems that arose in his community after his death. Given his authority among the believers, his words could be accepted and followed without question.

Unfortunately, his discourses were preserved only in the memories of the believers. When the time came to collect these memories, enormous difficulties ensued. By no means the least daunting was the fact that the believers who for one reason or another possessed the requisite information were scattered throughout the empire. It was necessary to go and seek them out, and thus the hunt for Hadith was on, a hunt of vast dimensions that was to last for several centuries. One had to think only of the number of dead Hadith scholars, and then consider that all the material they had collected amounted to nothing compared to that which remained to be discovered! Scholars of many nations have embarked on voyages to recover a scrap of language, unearth a manuscript, copy a book, or decipher a passage of sacred script. However, I think it would be difficult to find anything equivalent to the quest carried out by the Muslim Hadith scholars with the goal of collecting all the documents relating to one man (the Prophet), all the evidence of his acts and gestures, all the details—even the most trivial in appearance—of his life, and all the statements he ever made, in public or in private.

The quest was by no means easy. Many believers had succumbed to the temptation to use the authority of the Prophet to shore up texts that they then used to further personal interests or settle partisan disputes, and so false Hadiths proliferated. Given that Islam considers the deeds and words of the "Messenger of God" the model for the regulation of every detail of the believer's life, one can understand how much outrage the onslaught of apocryphal Hadiths could provoke. To be acceptable, an opinion had to rest upon the authority of the Qur'an or the Prophet; numerous disputes over dogma, jurisprudence, and political organization could be settled by invoking Prophetic Hadith. But a great many fabrications had crept into the corpus, and it fell to the vigilant guardians of the Hadith to spot them and denounce the men who had propagated them. But how to proceed?

Long and painstaking study of Hadiths both authentic and apocryphal had given some of the scholars a sixth sense for distinguishing between the two. This sense resembles the intuition that enabled the critic of poetry to sniff out a badly constructed verse. Besides this rather vague standard, one could also study the text of the Hadith itself and search for weaknesses in it. However, the scholars expended relatively little effort in this direction. From time to time, of course, they would discover an absurdity in the text of the Hadith, or some other characteristic that revealed the text as counterfeit and the attribution as fraudulent. But such cases occurred only as the result of some failure on the part of the inventor. The best forgers knew how to cover their tracks. One could hold their inventions up to the light and examine them from any angle without detecting a trace of their apocryphal character.

To expose forgeries, scholars opted for another procedure. The authenticity of a Hadith was to depend on its transmitters' reputation for moral integrity. An entire branch of the "Hadith sciences" thus came into being to deal with the narrators or "carriers" of the accounts, men whose credibility was to depend upon their veracity, orthodoxy, and religious zeal. Conversely, the testimony of anyone suspected of invoking the Prophet's authority to serve factional or private interests was to be rejected.

This procedure exerts an effect upon the form of the texts themselves. The Hadith text must originate with the Prophet and be correctly transmitted by a series of upstanding and blameless individuals. A Hadith, then, necessarily consists of two parts: the *matn* or actual utterance of the Prophet, and the *sanad* or chain of witnesses, that is, the unbroken sequence of trustworthy transmitters, culminating in the name of the Prophet. The text of the Hadith may be represented thus:

chain of witnesses——the name of the Prophet——the Prophet's actual utterance

Transmission

To verify a chain of transmitters, the Hadith scholars examine each of its links. After ascertaining that each of the transmitters of the Hadith actually knew his predecessor, they move on to the next stage of the critique: the testing of the veracity of the various witnesses. When both conditions are fulfilled, the Hadith is judged admissible, particularly when it is backed up by a second, independent chain of transmitters. The more numerous the chains, the more trustworthy the Hadith.

The acceptability of a Hadith depends on the credibility of its transmitters. Parallel to the hunt for Prophetic Hadiths runs the painstaking and mistrustful examination of the individuals who reported them. Suspicion is generalized and raised into a system; the innermost recesses of the transmitter's life and personality are ransacked and explored. It is no easy task, transmitters being as numerous as grains of sand. Every listener is a potential transmitter, so long as the utterance was pronounced in his presence. He is moreover bound to report any utterance traceable directly or indirectly to the Prophet and that, as a consequence, concerns the community. The capacity of the transmitter is accorded in principle to anyone with knowledge of a Hadith who can cite his sources and furnish proof of his integrity.

A transmitter must be a Muslim (adherents of other faiths are for all practical purposes enemies of Islam, even if no evidence to that effect exists in any given case). He or she must be an adult of sound mind: children and lunatics, being irresponsible, are never permitted to transmit.[2] The scholars differ on the status of heretics, but, in general, they consider a heretic's Hadith acceptable so long as it does not confirm the heresy in question. When it does, it is inadmissible.[3] Furthermore, a transmitter must be known for his sobriety and gravity; a man who passes his time telling jokes is considered likely to lie and thus also to perpetrate a forgery. As for habitual liars, they are summarily excluded: their taste for mendacity might well lead them to invent a false Hadith. To be certified, a transmitter must also be known to comport himself with dignity in everyday life.[4] If he eats in the marketplace or urinates in the street, for example, he places himself among the common mass of uneducated vulgarians, bereft of faith and law, and furnishes proof that he lacks the scruples that might deter him from falsehood.

Besides veracity and integrity, a transmitter must satisfy another, equally important obligation: he must exercise precision and exactitude *(dabt)* to prevent the Hadith from becoming distorted or curtailed. A transmitter must have a good memory; should he appear forgetful or careless, he loses his credibility.[5] To test his competence, the scholars recite a Hadith and tell him that he himself transmitted it. Should he be fooled, he is irretrievably discredited. But what happens when a transmitter forgets a Hadith he actually did transmit? Here is the answer of Ibn Qutayba (ninth century): "It may happen that a man forgets a Hadith he once transmitted, but which someone else remembers. Should someone remind him of it, he cannot remember it; but when he is told that he himself was the [original] transmitter, he retransmits it on the authority of the person who reminded him of it."[6] In other words, he becomes the transmitter of his own transmitter.

The chain of authorities is evidently no less important than the utterance itself, because, without the former, one can reach no verdict on the authenticity of the latter. The chain stands in the same relation to the text as do "legs in relation to the body."[7] A Hadith without its *sanad* is a body without legs: it can neither stand nor move. Deformed and mutilated, it lies helplessly on the ground where it fell.

Of course, right beside the Hadiths that walk proudly and firmly on two legs, we find the lame, the clubfooted, the one-legged, and the altogether legless. Similarly, each transmitter's attribute indicates the steadiness of his gait and the fate of the messages he carries. Besides the "solid" and "authoritative" transmitter, we find the "reliable" and "unobjectionable" one who "does not lie"; and then the "weak," "lying" transmitter "whose Hadiths are to be abandoned."[8]

The Liars

What becomes of rejected Hadiths? Instead of being destroyed, they are preserved—by the very same scholars who first decided they were forged of whole cloth. Too many copies have already spread, and even if one could destroy them all, the memory of them might one day resurface in the minds of those people who once knew them well. Side by side, therefore, with the canonical collections of authenticated Hadiths, we find the collections of apocryphal ones.

Among the latter is Ibn al-Jawzi's *Book of Forged Hadiths* (twelfth century), which contains plentiful information on the activities and motives of the forgers. It is not surprising to learn that persons holding beliefs foreign to Islam, or belonging to one dissident sect or another, forge Hadiths to support their own ideas. Nor is it surprising to find courtiers inventing Hadiths to legitimate their sovereign, or simply to flatter him. To a caliph fond of pigeons, a courtier recites a Hadith in which the Prophet praises pigeons. Unexpected, however, is the fact that even persons with praiseworthy intentions did not hesitate to forge Hadiths. A believer distressed by the people's neglect of the Qur'an circulates a Hadith enumerating the heavenly rewards promised to those people who read the Qur'an. Piety and virtue are no guarantee against falsehood; no one, it turns out, is a bigger liar than an ascetic. Ibn al-Jawzi also takes umbrage at popular preachers *(qussas)* who, in their efforts to please the crowd, shamelessly spread great numbers of apocryphal Hadiths. Veteran scholars have no trouble debunking them, but can do nothing to persuade a public eager for fantastic stories. It seems the storytellers even fabricate false chains of authorities. This trick can sometimes give rise to scenes out of a tale by Borges. One day Ibn Hanbal, one of Islam's greatest scholars, was forced to listen, dumbfounded and helpless, as a preacher regaled the crowd with an apocryphal Hadith attributed to . . . Ibn Hanbal! Besides the preachers, Ibn al-Jawzi mentions the forgers who, to lend weight to their opinions, answer questions only with Hadiths, as well as those forgers who attribute various statements to the Prophet with the object of giving themselves a reputation for knowing many Hadiths.[9]

False Hadiths require a full-fledged critical apparatus to brand the forgers. Ibn al-Jawzi examines the chain of transmitters and denounces the guilty parties, citing the judgments that reliable transmitters have passed against them.[10] The emphasis on transmitters does not, however, mean that the contents of the Hadith are passed over in silence. Take the case of a Hadith that claims that God created the horse, made it run, and then created himself from the horse's sweat. Examining the chain, Ibn al-Jawzi sniffs out a forger ("he would invent fifty Hadiths for a dirham"), but this is only a means of confirming what the author already knows on the basis of the unbelievability of the statement itself. A Hadith must be transmitted by trustworthy persons, but its content must also be worthy of belief. If upstanding individuals state that a camel passed through the eye of a needle, their reliability cannot change the fact that the claim itself is absurd. Ibn al-Jawzi concludes: "If you see that a Hadith contravenes reason *(al-ma'qul,)* or violates first principles *(al-usul)*, know that it is false." Such is the case with Hadiths that contradict the idea of divine transcendence by representing God anthropomorphically, or report facts inconsistent with the customs of the Prophet's time, such as the account that claims to preserve statements made by the Prophet in a public bath even though no such institution existed at the time.[11] In fact, real difficulties arise only in the case of Hadiths whose contents are believable and in accordance with the evidence of reason and the dictates of faith. To determine the authenticity of such Hadiths, one has no choice but to refer, as a last resort, to the chain of authorities.

According to Ibn al-Jawzi, a liar will sooner or later give himself away. Moreover, the author adds, people's hearts will naturally reject a lie. It should therefore suffice to listen to one's heart in order to tell true Hadiths from false. Ibn al-Jawzi cites a scholar who claims: "If a man decides at dawn to forge a Hadith, people will awaken with the knowledge that he is a liar." Nevertheless, Ibn al-Jawzi himself spent thirty years carrying out the prescriptions of a Hadith that turned out to be apocryphal![12] If liars could be exposed so easily, Ibn al-Jawzi would not have written his book.

In any event, the forger knows himself to be under constant surveillance. Sometimes, for fear of the Hellfire he is told awaits him after death, he makes amends for his crimes. Ibn al-Jawzi mentions certain persons who repented while ill, or on pilgrimage to Mecca. But repentance does not solve the whole problem. The apocryphal Hadiths have already passed from speakers to listeners, spreading like a contagion, and the penitent forger lies helplessly on his deathbed, unable to go back and catch his Hadith.[13] It will be a very long time before they fall into oblivion. Fortunately, works such as Ibn al-Jawzi's take up the task of decrying them (paradoxically, the way to

CHAPTER FIVE

Poetry and Coin

Indeterminacy

The ode of 'Antara, whose first verse I have already discussed, forms part of a group of seven (or ten) pre-Islamic poems known as the "Hanging Odes" *(al-mu'allaqat)*.[1] In an age when writing was crude and little practiced, these poems were written out and then suspended in the sanctuary at Mecca. They were also called the "Golden Odes," because they were written in letters of gold. Visitors circling the sanctuary could gaze up at the magnificent gilded inscriptions, and people who could read would distinguish in the sun-bright odes the words of the tribe transmuted into gold.

All this, it appears, is pure legend. Various historians state that the pre-Islamic odes (whose quality and influence on later Arabic poetry remain uncontested) were neither suspended nor gilded. Moreover, they were not composed before the appearance of Islam, at least not in their entirety, but rather at a much later period. The historians even go so far as to say that some of the poets credited with composing the odes never existed. Their biographies are the products of imagination, and the tales told of them merit no credence whatsoever.

Since the last century, historians have questioned the authenticity not only of the "Hanging Odes" but also of the entire corpus of pre-Islamic poetry. "Aside from a certain number of obvious cases, any attempt to distinguish the apocryphal from the authentic in so-called 'pre-Islamic poetry' is hopeless."[2] The "obvious cases" are the ones containing some feature or other that betrays the inauthenticity of the text, or poems deemed forgeries by the ancient Arabic philologists. The rest, by far the majority, contain no determining evidence one way or the other. We know some of them must be genuine, but they look as alike as black cats in the dark. Faced with this mass of material, the historian cannot dismiss the entire corpus of pre-Islamic poetry without throwing away the baby along with the bathwater. If there were "obvious cases" of authentic poems, the problem would be easier: there is certainly a better chance of identifying the false coins on the basis of the genuine ones than the other way around.

In this connection, a historian of literature writes: "A pastiche must be in effect more authentic than the original. To distinguish the pastiches amid the mass of so-called pre-Islamic poetry, we must first identify an indisputably genuine work to serve as a standard. However, it is precisely such a work that we lack."[3] Like any imitation, a forgery requires a model. Although it comes after the original, the forgery conceals its derivativeness by passing for the model itself. In his own way, the forger maintains the strictest deference to the original, reproducing its style in the tiniest detail. When he succeeds, confusion follows, and the reaper proves incapable of separating the wheat from the chaff.

The historian cannot even invoke an aesthetic criterion. To say that genuine poems possess a discernible "spontaneity" and the apocryphal ones an equally discernible "artificiality" is to attribute a mythical value to origins and to primal energies. Such a claim ignores the constraints imposed by the poetic tradition, constraints that no era, no matter how far back, has ever escaped. Most of all, it underestimates the forgers, who sometimes mastered poetic technique as fully as their models ever did, and who, like many imitators, eventually surpassed their predecessors.

Whom to trust? Nothing separates the good from the wicked, or the innocent from the guilty. Every "pre-Islamic" poem displays the same air of indifference and impassivity. The historian-detective will never succeed in passing judgment on them all, and the historian-gardener will never succeed in clearing the field of all the weeds that have flourished in secret for so long. He can treat the whole matter ironically, or express astonishment at the massive fraud perpetrated in ancient times and still in force today. But if he wants to "use" the "pre-Islamic" corpus, he has no choice but to accept whatever the ancient transmitters have passed on. He will of course note that the corpus is unreliable, and that caution is necessary when dealing with accounts of the archaic poets. Yet his method will not differ fundamentally from that of the Arabic philologists of the eighth and ninth centuries who collected, compiled, and recorded "pre-Islamic" poetry, and who in the course of their work came to investigate the problem of forgery.

The Money Changer

Two main causes prompted the philologists to take an interest in pre-Islamic poetry. The first was the necessity of ironing out linguistic difficulties in the Qur'an, and the second was the feeling that poetry was the irreplaceable record *(diwan)* of all that concerned the ancient Arabs. To save the memory from oblivion, it was necessary to master poetry.

Every great pre-Islamic poet had his transmitter *(rawi),* usually an apprentice poet entrusted with recording (usually in his memory) and then propagating his master's poems. Before being fixed in writing, ancient poetry circulated orally in this manner. This type of transmission drove philologists to despair. The same poem appeared in different versions, the order of verses varied from one version to another, attributions were uncertain, and names coincided (for example, a dozen different poets were all named Imru'ul-Qays).[4] Over and above all these problems, forgeries proliferated. Tribal spirit and political and religious dissension prompted individuals or groups to place poems in the mouths of archaic poets. To prove the pedigree of a rule of grammar, grammarians all too eagerly forged their own "pre-Islamic" verses.[5]

In collecting ancient poems, the philologists by and large adopted the methods of the Hadith specialists.[6] To achieve recognition and legitimacy, a poem needed the backing of the scholars. One day an amateur told the eighth-century scholar Khalaf, "When I hear a poem I like, I couldn't care less what you and your colleagues have to say about it." Retorted Khalaf: "If you found a dirham and liked it, and a money changer told you it was debased, what good would your approval do you then?"[7] In all matters of poetry, the connoisseur is an assayer schooled in the varieties of coinage and the rates of exchange. His judgment is final: the coin he rejects will sooner or later find itself taken out of circulation.

But the money changer may be a forger too, and the assayer may pass out counterfeit coin. Khalaf, who seemed so conscientious in the passage just cited, along with his contemporary Hammad the Transmitter, were some of the greatest forgers Arab culture has ever known. Certainly an unscrupulous money changer would be swiftly denounced by his colleagues. But when the market became infested with forgers, suspicion fell indiscriminately upon the money changers one and all.

Reception of the Poem

One might object that these questions are secondary. It is futile to waste time over disputed attributions because, forged or not, "pre-Islamic" poems possess undeniable artistic value. One might add that precisely because of its ahistoricity, the corpus frees us from a documentary approach to the tradition and instead invites us to consider the poems in their own right and for their own sake. We do not know whether they were written in the sixth century or the eighth, but we know they have intrinsic value above and beyond their subordination to one author or another.[8] Even while denying any concession to "aestheticism" and signaling in passing the necessity for "historically informed reading," an Arabist says of the "Hanging Odes":

> Both the passionate effusions and the naturalistic descriptions glow with an intensity we can attribute to an originary time and place or, should we choose, to a talent for reconstruction. What real difference does it make to us whether it is a sixth-century nomad or a Basran or Kufan litterateur who sings of the breathless joys of the lover-thief . . . or the swaying ride through the desert, and the mirage that shimmers over the burning dunes. . . ? One way or the other, a great voice has spoken.[9]

This pronouncement gives us two ways to read the Hanging Odes: for scholarship or for pleasure. Or, put differently, there are two levels to the poem: a historical level, where a relationship exists between the text and its psychological and sociological context; and a poetic level, constructed around a kernel of inalterable meaning above and beyond the identity of the poet. At this second level, the text leads a life of its own and asserts itself in isolation from any reference to whomever may have composed it. However, this distinction seems to me somewhat arbitrary. Does it really not matter to the reader whether a camel-riding nomad or a jaded city dweller composed a description of the desert? Whether learned or untutored, the reading of a poem presupposes a more-or-less precise conception of the author. Reading bases itself on whatever preconception one may have of the author. Where knowledge is lacking, imagination will fill the gap. A closed text is one that offers no such latitude, but closed texts are monsters of the sort no one has ever actually seen.

The reader's attitude toward a poem changes when he or she learns that the poem is genuine, or that it is not. Because they scramble labels and multiply images, forgeries have a special appeal. Often a poem declines in value when shown to be a forgery (even though a forgery often recoups its value as it ages).[10] It is noteworthy that the pastiche and the forgery, no matter how well executed, hold only marginal status in the other genres. A pastiche can be a masterpiece of its genre, but never a masterpiece plain and simple. When produced by a great author, a forgery may well escape marginality, but it can never escape ambivalence. The shadow of the supposed author looms on the horizon and weighs down—or enriches—any interpretation of the work.

CHAPTER SIX

The Poetics of the Anecdote

Judgements apply only to the appearance of things. God does not demand that human beings judge of hidden natures or act on the basis of guesses about intentions. A man is judged a Muslim on the basis of his public profession of faith, even though he may disavow it in private. He is judged his father's son if he was born to his father's wife and is acknowledged as a son, even if his true father be someone altogether different.

—Al-Jahiz, "Epistle on Singing Girls"

"Straw man": one who acts in a certain matter in name only. "Prête-nom" : 1. One who appears to be the principal party in some transaction without being significantly involved, and signs an agreement whose principal contractor prefers not to appear. 2. One who lends his name to a work he has not composed, a statement he has not made, or the like.

—Littré, *Dictionnaire de la langue française* (1863)

Al-Jahiz, the Pig, and the Devil

Unlike the other animals, the pig, it seems, was not created on the sixth day. A diversity of creatures swarmed over land, sea, and air, but pigs were nowhere to be found. In fact, such beasts came into being only because human beings sinned and God punished them by transforming them into pigs. This chastisement was terrible, according to the ninth-century writer al-Jahiz, who notes that if ugliness itself could take on physical form, the result could be no less horrifying than a pig.[1] This animal, carefully considered, is disturbing: it was once a human being, with men and women for ancestors! This statement may explain the aversion of entire peoples to eating pork, which must surely still contain some trace of human flesh.

The pig's metamorphosis is irreversible and final. Stories often show us evil genies and wicked sorcerers transforming people into monkeys or statues of bronze or marble. However, the victims generally revert to human form by the end of the story. On the other hand, the pig will always be a pig. Furthermore, its transformation is so thorough that it retains no memory of its former state—of its humanity, now lost forever. This fact too sets it apart from the heroes of tales who, even though enchanted, keep their memory and sometimes even their ability to speak or, failing that, to write. But the pig does not know, nor will it ever know, that it was once a human being.

Nevertheless, the pig still falls short of being supremely ugly. Perhaps its punishment was insufficient and still has further to fall along the scale of abominations, or perhaps it can find among God's creatures a being even more abject than itself. Indeed, by some inexplicable chance, there once lived a man more repulsive than the pig. This man, known as al-Jahiz (ninth century),[2] was described by a rhymester as follows:

> Transmute a pig to an uglier form!
> He could ne'er with al-Jahiz vie;

If you look at him, you look on Hell
With a splinter in your eye.[3]

Al-Jahiz has reached the highest degree of ugliness. God was actually merciful to the pig, for he could have made it look like al-Jahiz and thus rendered it even more hideous. Contemplating the pig, al-Jahiz sees his own image, or rather a corrected and improved version of himself. The very sight of al-Jahiz's face is intolerable and may lead to blindness ("a splinter in the eye"). All told, his face is a vision of Hell; and when Hell is mentioned, the Devil cannot be far behind.

Ancient Arabic authors have no faces. For religious reasons, painting and representational art in general had a poor reputation. No one made efforts to have his image preserved in paint and canvas. For this reason, it is strictly impossible to imagine the men and women of long ago. Despite this limitation, certain modern authors have attempted to sketch tentative portraits on the basis of a few literary references.[4] Given the absence of a model, of course, the results are hardly reliable. We know that al-Jahiz was short and had dark skin and bulging eyes, but such features alone cannot construct an individual face or figure. We also know that his appearance was repulsive, but there are many types of ugliness, and no amount of shrewd guessing can tell us exactly what his may have been.[5]

However, we have at least one model for our sketch. Al-Jahiz, we are told, was as ugly as the Devil. Paint the Devil, and you will have painted al-Jahiz. Of course, we must first be able to capture the image of the Devil. This task is not easy, because the Devil must appear in order to be depicted. At least we have to know whom (or what) he resembles so as to have at hand some of the features that distinguish him. Because we are dealing with an invisible entity, we have to imagine his features, to the extent that the invisible can be imagined. Taking into account that the Devil represents the supreme degree of ugliness, we must paint the most repulsive possible visage. But once again, there are many ways to depict ugliness. Fortunately, we know the Devil resembles al-Jahiz. If we paint the one, we will have painted the other. The circularity is perfect, and brings us to the anecdote of the woman who wanted to have the image of the Devil carved onto a piece of jewelry. When the engraver could not find a model, the woman went out into the street and, catching sight of al-Jahiz, brought him into the shop and said, "Like him!"

Al-Jahiz is the image of the Devil; he stands for the Devil; he is the Devil. If he was chosen from among all the creatures passing in the street, it is because his affinity to the Devil renders him capable of serving as a model for him. The woman, moreover, did not want al-Jahiz's image carved on her jewelry, but the Devil's. In pointing out al-Jahiz, she pointed out the Devil.[6] When she shows the piece to her friends, she will breathe no word of al-Jahiz (whose name she does not even know). She will simply show them the image of the Devil, which they will regard as carved on the model of the Devil, not on the model of a man who happens to resemble him. Smiling and vaguely uneasy, the woman will speak the name of the Devil.

This anecdote would not surprise readers because the story fits al-Jahiz. As for al-Jahiz himself, he goes on to speak of the rules to be followed when inventing an anecdote or presenting a text under an assumed name. Before examining his reflections on this question, it will be of interest to look at how the idea of "appropriateness" was expressed in the case of erotic poetry.

The Onomastics of Love

The poet Jamil devoted the majority of his poems to a woman called Buthayna. He was called Jamil of Buthayna, and their two names became as inseparable as Tristan and Isolde or Abelard and Heloise. Jamil never possessed Buthayna, yet he did possess her—in name only.

Her name became his property,[7] and any other poet's use of it would be a usurpation. Thus anyone wishing to put verses in Jamil's mouth had only to slip in the name "Buthayna." The audience, familiar with the connection between the two, would never guess that the poem was a forgery.

This connection does not apply to all names. Some had no predetermined place—that is, no privileged link to a poet—and were available to be served up over and over again. They constituted a repertoire from which a poet could choose (often on the basis of rhyme or meter) whichever suited him. Poets were nevertheless to avoid using clumsy or awkward names such as "Bawza'." Yet what makes such a name clumsy and awkward is its failure to belong to a poetic domain that admits only a finite and restricted number of names—most commonly Layla, Hind, and Fatima. These names, says Ibn Rashiq, are "sweet on the tongue." We understand him to mean that their pleasant associations derive from the poetic context in which they most frequently appear. If the poet's beloved has an unpoetic name, he must change it in order to elicit a favorable response from his audience. To mention Layla is to cite by implication all the poems where the name appears, and to signal one's continuity with a tradition. For this reason, proper names come to function as common nouns. Instead of designating any particular woman, they become emblems that designate the whole genre of erotic poetry. To better affirm his connection to the tradition, the poet may even cite several such names in a single poem.[8]

This fact may well surprise those readers who imagine that a love poem addresses a woman, and only one at that. They may ask whether the different names mentioned in the poem are all pseudonyms of the same person or whether the poet is unfaithful in his affections. These questions arise from a naive belief that a love poem is supposed to express the poet's feelings.[9] No such idea detained the critics of Arabic poetry. They pose the question only to deny its importance, declaring it a tiresome exercise because the sincerity of a speaker can never be known through a text.[10]

One may claim that the poet nevertheless presents an image of himself and his beloved. However, this image is hardly personal. The poet's reported speech as well as the woman's (when the poem contains dialogue) follow precise rules. This delightful comment by Ibn Rashiq proves the point: "In Arab custom, the poet is the languishing lover. Among other nations, however, the woman is depicted as taking the initiative and seeking to address the poet. This attests to the nobility of the Arabs and their zeal in guarding their womenfolk."[11] In other words, it is the man's role to display desire, and the woman's to deny it. It follows that a woman, in principle, can never compose a love poem. As the object of erotic discourse, she cannot be its subject because initiative properly falls to the man. The poet is committed to attribute to her whatever discourse "custom" dictates, which in this case amounts to rebuffing the lover's advances. This discourse is the only one appropriate to her womanly status. The poet must redouble his efforts to seduce the woman, whereas she must remain obdurate in the face of his advances. In the end, the love poem tells the tale of an unshared passion.

Whenever a rule of this type exists, someone will inevitably come along to subvert it. The perpetrator in this case is the seventh-century poet Ibn Abi Rabiʻa, who reverses the roles and depicts himself as an object of feminine desire. Instead of rebuffing him as custom demands, women actively pursue him.[12] To the women courting him he attributes speeches that fail to conform to the role tradition has fixed for them. His verses, accepted as violations of the rules, actually emphasize them, as is often the case with exceptions.

Convention does not apply only to the depiction of women. It also manifests itself when the poet speaks of his own body. The poet must be emaciated, sleepless, and frail. One poet describes himself thus: "Inside my clothing is a wasted body; if you leaned upon it, it would collapse." The poet who spoke these lines, as it happens, was obese. A disjunction clearly exists between the physical reality of his body and the words he uses to describe it. Measured against the body, the verse seems to fall short in two ways. Not only is the poet himself fat, but he may be lying about his passion the same way he lied about his corpulence.[13] The poet's body betrays him and reveals the convention. A poet can tailor his language however he wishes, but he can never tailor his body to fit his language. In this way, erotic poetry constitutes a "regulated imposture," all because of fidelity to the tradition, that is, to the antecedent poetic corpus. In sum, the poet is in love only with the women beloved by his predecessors.

The Salt of Baptism

In his *Book of Misers,* al-Jahiz makes a number of remarks on forgery. He is concerned with the question of anecdotes, specifically with the possibility of reporting an incident and mentioning the name of the protagonist. "We have recorded for you many stories with attributions to the persons involved, but in many cases we have suppressed the attribution, either out of fear of those persons, or out of a desire to protect them."[14] This concern for the protagonist's name suggests a link between the narration of an incident and the identity of the person involved. For al-Jahiz, there are two types of anecdotes, which we may label "opaque" and "transparent."

"Opaque" anecdotes contain no hint or clue that would permit one to recognize or identify the hero. Al-Jahiz does not hesitate to report such stories. Even when their heroes are known through some other source, they remain inaccessible. The resulting anecdotes are somehow curled up inside themselves. They enclose the set of elements that construct them and leave no door open to the outside world. They are, in a word, miserly. No centrifugal force can tear them free of the circular play of signs and compel them to reveal the identity of whomever it was that gave rise to them in the first place. Because they hang upon nothing external to themselves, al-Jahiz can place them in his work with impunity. However, he does so with a sulk, because such tales "can hardly be enjoyed without knowing the identity of the persons involved—that is, without being associated with fitting characters and likely protagonists. When their connection to their source is severed, the tales lose half their spice and freshness."[15]

The "spice" or "salt" of the tale owes much to the physical contact one can have with its characters. In this sense, there exists an inequality between al-Jahiz, who knows the background of the stories he reports, and the real reader, who lacks any such knowledge and is reduced to dealing with the text and the text alone.

No such inequality exists in the case of the second type, the transparent anecdote. This type presents a personality familiar to both author and reader. Like a clay jug that allows water to transpire through its pores, the transparent anecdote leaves no doubt as to the identity of the persons involved, even when it avoids actually naming them, or conceals their identity behind a paraphrase or pseudonym: "There are stories here which, from the very first syllable, expose the persons involved, even when we have not named them explicitly, nor wish them to be named. Since entertaining you is not worth harming them, this category of anecdotes had to dropped altogether, leaving a great but unavoidable gap in the present work; for this section was the longest and the likeliest to have pleased you."[16]

Transparent anecdotes possess so great an anaphoric power that the author can do nothing to stop them from bringing a name to the lips of the reader. Certain actions and statements, it seems, are so closely associated with one subject that the mere mention of them instantly betrays the identity of that subject. Particular attributes of the story point to an anchoring name, and the recognition of that name not only heightens the power of the anecdote but also opens up a vast field of related anecdotes, all of which have the same figure as their hero.

The opaque anecdote leads a life of its own, but it is a threadbare, reduced, and ultimately sterile life that cannot extend beyond itself. On the other hand, the transparent anecdote, albeit modestly concealed behind a veil, knows no restraint. Replete and generous, it flaunts its connections in such a way as to provoke interest and covert delight on the part of the observer.

Besides these two types of anecdote, there is also the "exemplary anecdote." This type depicts a character whose name, by some subtle transformation, becomes the sign of a moral quality or other attribute such as beauty, stupidity, generosity, or stinginess. The actions and statements attributed to such a character conform to and extend the function he exemplifies, and prepare the ground for a proliferation of numberless bastard offspring. Once this proliferation has begun, no standard permits us to distinguish between legitimate and bastard children:

> We have never seen a community condemn or despise a man for going beyond generosity to the point of prodigal excess. Rather, we find him studied, admired, and emulated, even to the extent that he is given credit for feats of generosity he never performed and has attributed to him marvels of charity greater than any he actually achieved. . . . All anonymous acts of kindness are deemed his, and all praises of generosity are eventually supposed to have been composed originally for him. Moreover, we find the very same community treating the miser in precisely contrary fashion. . . . They hate and despise him, extend their enmity to his descendants and his clan, and attach to his name feats of meanness he never performed, and marvels of stinginess he never achieved.[17]

As the standard by which moral character is judged, the exemplary figure possesses an irresistible voracity. It engulfs everything inside the space it controls. It is an empty shell with a yawning mouth, filling itself with whatever new content it can swallow, the new content being always reminiscent of the old. This repletion permits a certain rhetorical concision. Because he is familiar to both author and reader, the exemplary figure can be evoked with the most sparing of details. His name refers directly to an instantly recognizable background. Like the transparent anecdote, the exemplary anecdote permits the construction of a series of tales featuring the same protagonist; it wears a sort of cloak that can be stretched in any direction. No attribution of words or actions to the exemplar can ever have unpleasant consequences, either for the exemplar or for the person making the attribution. The salient property of the figure is its transcendence of time and place.[18] Joseph is always beautiful, and Nestor was never young.

Tellers of anecdotes and forgers of all sorts must obey certain rules. First, they must follow certain stylistic conventions. Al-Jahiz mentions them in passing: "If you find vulgar, improper, or grammatically incorrect language in this book, you should know that I have included it intentionally because pedantry spoils this sort of anecdote by distancing it from its actual circumstances. The exceptions occur when I cite tales of seemingly intelligent misers and scholarly pinchpennies, like Sahl b. Harun."[19]

Elevated style is appropriate only when the character in the story belongs to the class of eloquent speakers. Otherwise, low style is called for. In either case, the choice of style depends upon the image of the person whose speech one wishes to reproduce. Furthermore, the choice of characters follows rules of appropriateness as well. The success of an anecdote depends upon it: "If you tell an anecdote and attach it to Abu al-Harith Jummayn, al-Haytham b. Mutahhar, Muzabbad, or Ibn Ahmar, it will succeed even if it is a tepid story. Conversely, if you make up a zesty and piquant anecdote and apply it to Salih b. Hunayn, Ibn al-Nawwa', or some other repellent personality, it will suddenly become tedious—and a tedious anecdote is worse than a tepid one."[20]

The "zestiness" or "tepidity" of an anecdote is a direct result of the choice made about the individual with whom it is associated. The name chosen will effectively determine the reader's attitude toward the story. If the name belongs to an individual known for his buffoonery, the story will immediately evoke a set of appropriate associations. A familiar horizon emerges against which the suddenly compliant reader can accept whatever the story says. When he does, the story itself acquires value. On the other hand, when the anecdote is attributed to "a repellent personality," the reader's attention wavers—or, rather, he finds himself unwilling to consider the story worthwhile. This reaction occurs independently of any intrinsic value the anecdote may possess.

This pattern holds true for other genres as well. For example, sermons derive their power not only from their solemn and affecting style, but also from the speaker to whom they are attributed. Al-Jahiz notes that the reception of a sermon depends on whether it is attributed to an ascetic or to a libertine:

> If you compose an exhortation in praise of asceticism and say, "This is a sermon by Bakr b. 'Abd Allah al-Muzani, or 'Amir b. 'Abd Qays al-'Anbari, or Muriq al-'Ijli, or Yazid al-Raqqashi," its appeal will double because the attribution will lend it a freshness and loftiness it does not possess. But if you say, "This is a sermon by Abu Bakr al-Sufi, or 'Abd al-Mu'min, or the poet Abu Nuwas, or the libertine Husayn," it will have to succeed on its own merits, and the likeliest result is that people will deny it any value at all.[21]

The same discourse possesses differential value depending on the person given credit for it.[22] Thus it is essential to choose that person carefully, as the choice will determine the reader's response to the text. In general, an utterance within any literary genre provokes a certain distress: a sort of anxious and suspenseful readiness to pounce upon the text with a judgment. Only the imposition of a name can relieve the suspense by pinning a meaning to the text. This process assumes that an utterance deprived of an author is dangerous—an unfamiliar region where the reader stands uncertain of which path to take, or wanders aimlessly in search of some familiar point of reference.

Taking all these factors into account, we may say that readers confronted with a new text must take their bearings twice. First, they must take note of the stylistic features that indicate the text's membership in a genre. Doing so reduces the play of meaning to a manageable level. But even with this attribution to anchor it, the text still drifts at the mercy of the wind and the current. The mesmerizing ebb and flow of meaning and the seasickness that follows will stop only with the second operation, namely, steering the text toward an author who stands on the terra firma of a familiar shore where all the paths lead to places one has already visited.

Every genre is built around a constellation of names. Any utterance inscribed within the purview of a particular genre should be attributed to only one of the names that form the constellation. These names—interchangeable among themselves—form a metonymic link to the genre; indeed, they are its essential constituent. Should they be obscured, the text loses its credibility because it derives its value from their presence.

It follows, then, that an author cannot escape the genre where he first dropped anchor and where conventional wisdom has imprisoned him. He is forbidden to move elsewhere. No matter that he is capable of reproducing himself at will within his genre, or that any new text within the genre can be attributed to him; he resists being transplanted to a foreign soil where his coin has no currency. He lives on an isolated planet with its own elements, gravity, and laws of motion. If forced to move to another planet, he flounders in an unbreathable atmosphere and floats in space, unable to cling to any fixed object. One cannot attribute to a generous man the traits of a miser; in the same way, one cannot credit an author famous for debauchery with an edifying sermon. Moreover, any such attribution will arouse the suspicion of the reader, who will wonder whether we are trying to trick

him by presenting him with an apocryphal text. No forger can afford
to commit this kind of error. If he does, he will see the effect he has
worked to achieve come to nothing in the face of the reader's doubt
and, eventually, his unwillingness even to consider the text. For readers, ascetics never tell jokes and libertines never give sermons.[23]

Of course, there are always exceptions to the rule. For example,
"the poet Abu Nuwas" did compose a number of moralizing poems.
However, he is not famous for them. In al-Jahiz's time as well as our
own, Abu Nuwas figures as a dissipated libertine who frequented tav-
erns and praised the beauty of young men. He has been fixed inside a
stereotype closed to any anomalies that might spoil his pure exem-
plarity. We can therefore credit him with bacchic verse and off-color
jokes, but never with a discourse on asceticism. If one tried to credit
him with a sermon, readers would respond in one of two ways: they
would regard the text either as a fake or as an irreverent parody. Either way, they would recoil from the conjunction of opposites and
condemn the text as an unwarranted irruption of scandal into a pri-
vately owned territory closed off to intruders.

The True Author

The exemplary name travels as a captive along a discursive route that
it is powerless to alter. The same is not true, however, of the forger,
who presides over the game and pulls the strings from somewhere
offstage. Far from being the prisoner of genre, the forger or *real author* (a term we will refine in a moment) can leap mischievously from
one genre to another. He can pilfer any treasure with a casualness
born of instinctive mastery of texts and the rules of attribution. Nevertheless, he remains an ambiguous figure. He is the occasion, or the
pretext, for a text that someone else could well have produced, and

that therefore should be attributed to that speaker. False as he is, the forger is still the *real* author. But only the pseudoauthor, the assumed name, is the *true* author. Only he can claim the title of author—the first, originary, and unquestioned source. By disguising himself and his deception, the forger is both an essential appendage and a parasitical growth—a sort of gadfly in disguise.

As al-Jahiz's text indicates, both the sermon and the humorous anecdote are associated with a number of exemplary names. However, this number is limited. Forgers, on the other hand, are legion. Anyone can compose a text—even al-Jahiz's own reader ("If *you* compose an exhortation . . ."). A forger must only remember to place his text under a name that will confer authority upon it. Any reader can put words and sentences together as he likes, but the result will be acceptable only if he tacks on an appropriate name. In this way, texts can multiply at will, but the number of authors must remain fixed. Every genre is buoyed up by those names that alone can grant admission to a new text, all by virtue of their contextual familiarity. In the final analysis, the practice of fraudulent attribution serves as a sort of homage rendered to a past studded with prestigious authors whose example—whose discourse—must be perpetuated.

A forged text faces in two directions at once. It looks to the real author on the one hand, and to the true author on the other. The actual author must efface himself in favor of the true one. As a result, the reader can interpret the work in light of his image of the true author. Nevertheless, so long as there are two authors, there are also two texts—or, rather, two interpretations of the same text, depending on which author the reader has in mind. Of course, this kind of double interpretation is possible only if the fraud is discovered.

Under these conditions, the text cannot be considered as the *expression* of its two-headed author. On the one hand, the *real* author does not acknowledge it, at least not openly. Although he gave birth to it in the first place, he professes not to recognize it. In fact, he strives to quash any suspicion of his paternity. On the other hand, the *true* author, although he serves to authenticate the text, is not the only one who could do so. As we have seen in the cases of the anecdote and the sermon, several names can function equally well as the object of attribution. The text can migrate to another author without posing a problem for interpretation, so long as both candidates hold exemplary status within the genre.

CHAPTER SEVEN

Confessions of a Forger

Jealous Rivals

Many forgers never confessed to their crimes. Perhaps some of them admitted their guilt to friends who (as happens sometimes) kept the secret safe. A smaller number were unmasked by critics with a nose for trifling inconsistencies in the text or the alleged transmission. However, only a very few forgers confessed freely and openly to creating apocryphal texts. One who did was al-Jahiz, who admits to having attributed certain of his writings to past authors. The epistle that contains this admission [1] offers a great deal of insight into the composition and circulation of books in his time.

Books circulated by means of transmitters who copied a work at the author's dictation and then received an "authorization" to transmit it to others. No one could become a transmitter unless the author declared him worthy of the task. By obtaining his authorization, the transmitter acquired proprietary rights over the author's book. He was now qualified to use the work in his own teaching and to license others to transmit it. In this way, the number of transmitters multiplied. Furthermore, each one made it a point of honor to accumulate as many authorizations as possible. [2] At each presentation of a work, the transmitter had to mention not only the name of the author (the "father") but also the names of the tutors who had taught him the book. Publication often had unpleasant consequences for the author. Al-Jahiz knew what was in store for him every time he signed off on a new book: "Envious [critics] begin to jostle like rutting camels, hoping to discover some way of discrediting my book in the eyes of its patron." If the patron was "sharp-witted and perceptive," he would recognize the book's merits and dismiss the critics. But then the critics would resort to a second trick: "They steal the ideas out of the book, rewrite them, add some filler, and present their pirated version to another prince in order to win his favor. Of course, when [the original book] had my name on it, all they could do was criticize it."[3]

To publish a work is first to see it unfairly criticized and then shamelessly plagiarized. How was an author to avoid all this unpleasantness? The solution, as effective as it is radical, was to attribute it to an ancient and time-honored author:

> I would often compose a second book, inferior in form and content [to one I saw attacked], and attribute it to an author of the past, such as Ibn al-Muqaffaʿ, al-Khalil, Salm the head of the Caliphal Academy, Yahya b. Khalid, al-ʿAttabi, and the like. Then the very same people who criticized my first and better book would come to me asking after the second and inferior one. They would ask me to read it for them, and they would copy it all down by hand so they could study it among themselves. They would imitate it, quote it, cite it in their letters and speeches, teach it to others on my authority, and gain preeminence and popularity thereby, all because my name does not appear in it anywhere and no one attributes it to me.[4]

A contemporary author was a rival who must be cut down to size, but an ancient one was an authority who must be approached with fitting reverence. Because knowledge derived from dead authors, the reader always found a way to justify their errors and omissions. Besides, there was so much one could do with the work of a dead author. Readers had to recopy it and learn it from its transmitter (or pseudotransmitter), seek authorizations to teach it, and, most important, debate its meaning. Thanks to its appearance under the name of an illustrious forefather, the book was magically protected from self-serving critics and plagiarists.

Al-Jahiz thus avoided a good deal of trouble by resorting to a false attribution. Yet he was still not satisfied. Compared to the author, the transmitter was a minor figure. He may have been sought as a teacher and mentioned whenever the book was retransmitted, but he was given no "credit for originality";[5] it belonged to the author alone. Of course, al-Jahiz could console himself with the thought that he had fooled all his colleagues. He could also reassure himself that he wrote as well as the ancients. Only envy made the critics disparage the works he circulated under his own name—works that were actually better than the ones he palmed off on the ancients. Even so, he could enjoy success only by proxy. His secret knowledge of his own authorship, far from consoling him, made him only bitter. As the transmitter of his own work in disguise, he had to be satisfied with the feeble reflections of someone else's fame.

An easy way out would have been to stop writing. But al-Jahiz had too much to say. Besides, he earned his living by writing books. In the end, he found a solution that, without being perfect, was the least of all evils, and permitted him to escape both the attacks of his colleagues and the ravages of his predecessors. The solution was to attribute the text to an anonymous author:

Often, too, I have produced a book as firm and polished as a monument of stone, its ideas subtle and tightly intertwined and its language lofty and eloquent. I could not bear to see it attacked by envious critics, which would happen if I took the credit for it. Nor could I bear to give someone else the credit for its splendid structure and fine expressions. So I would present it to the public as an anonymous work—that is, as an ancient work of unknown authorship. And swarms of readers, as avid as racehorses on a track, would charge after it and vie with one another to obtain it.[6]

Despite having an anonymous author, al-Jahiz's publication met with approval. This fact may seem surprising at first, since we have already noted that a work commanded respect only when a celebrated author took responsibility for it. Yet al-Jahiz is careful to note that the book appears as an "*ancient* work of unknown authorship." The book may have been anonymous, but it was also ancient. On this assumption, it commanded respect. For whatever reason, ancient works were usually considered beyond dispute. Anonymity was not so critical a defect after all. As long as the text first saw the light of day in the originary "before-time," it made little difference that it could not be linked to a specific, well-known author.

Attributing his book to an anonymous author alleviated al-Jahiz's jealousy. Doubtless it did so because anonymity is ambiguous. Even though al-Jahiz had to renounce his book, he did not have to concede it to anyone in particular. Only this compromise could afford him peace of mind. He could even hope one day to claim the work as his own. An anonymous work is an orphan, and it is more plausible to claim to be the father of an orphan than of a child who already bears a father's name.

The Claim

Al-Jahiz actually did try to reclaim his works. At the end of his life, he set his house in order by acknowledging his natural children. We have no idea how his claims were received, although it is conceivable that they met with some serious opposition. By the time a book becomes successful and widely distributed, it is almost impossible to separate it from the name customarily attached to it. If someone claims to be its real author, he must prove his claim. Simply announcing oneself to be the author will not suffice.[7]

The problem is actually twofold. For one thing, al-Jahiz must admit the deception and explain precisely why he renounced his own works to begin with. For another, he must prove that he did in fact perpetrate a fraud. He must appeal to the testimony of persons who know the truth and who can attest to having seen his work before publication. That is, he must have a solid reputation as a forger. Furthermore, he must persuade his colleagues that he is not simply perpetrating some new fraud. This point is the touchiest of all. People approached him to hear his dictation of older works only because they judged him a reliable transmitter. Now that he has declared himself an imposter, he has lost all his credibility. How can one judge the sincerity of someone who claims to have been lying? It is impossible to tell whether the deception lies in the false attribution or in the eleventh-hour claim to paternity.[8]

Only the pseudoauthors—the "straw men"—can furnish real proof. Being of the "older generation," however, they cannot speak. It was precisely because of their being dead that al-Jahiz attributed his works to them in the first place.

This whole matter, disturbing as it is, undermines any convictions one may have about the authenticity of numerous classical works. In his confessions, al-Jahiz is neither cynical nor repentant. The literary practices of his era accepted misattribution as a necessary evil, albeit they did so with a vague sense of uneasiness. Al-Jahiz puts the blame for his premeditated fraud on his "envious critics." But for their scheming, he implies, he would have let the dead rest in peace.

A disguised work by al-Jahiz leads several lives in succession. First, it submits to transmission under a borrowed name. To perform the transmission successfully, al-Jahiz must take various precautions. He must choose a "straw author" who could have plausibly written a book on the subject at hand. He must not evince satisfaction or disappointment at the reactions of colleagues or copyists, and in general avoid, by look or word, any betrayal of the secret. Thanks to the transmitters, the book travels far and wide, all under the name of the pseudoauthor. Afterward, al-Jahiz decides to claim the work as his own. Having worked so hard to keep his name out of the matter, he must now strive to put it back in. Now he must rub out the name of the author who—through no fault of his own—has appropriated his book. For a while, people may attribute the work equally to the straw author and to al-Jahiz. One imagines that the dispute would come to an end with al-Jahiz's death. Rivalries end and jealousies lapse once our author becomes one of the "ancients" himself. He joins the cohort of all those celebrated writers whose names and reputations he appropriated. Once in their august company, he may well have some explaining to do: his generous gifts to them turned out to be a loan. Not only did he demand the books back, but he collected interest as well—lending false coin to be repaid in true.

Amid the pantheon of celebrities, al-Jahiz can defend himself by pointing out that he has succumbed to the same fate. After all, now he can be a straw man too. While alive, he did not foresee that people would one day attribute works to him that he never composed. God knows how he would have reacted had he come across a book falsely ascribed to himself!

The Mask

Al-Jahiz's confessions must have opened the eyes of a number of young writers. Al-Jahiz's own fate serves as an example of the result, or at least suggests that others followed his lead and began their careers by committing forgery. A number of works—for example, *Kitab al-taj* (The book of the crown) and *Kitab al-mahasin wa l-addad* (The book of antitheses)—have been attributed to him, although scholars have yet to decide the matter of their authorship with any certainty.

Kitab al-taj deals with court protocol. It appears to be the work of a forger who for unknown reasons never claimed it as his own. Although the matter has yet to be settled,[9] the style of the work strikes the reader as different from the characteristic style of al-Jahiz's authenticated works. There does exist an unmistakably Jahizian style, recognizable in the structure of sentences, the frequent digressions, a penchant for antithesis and hyperbole, and most of all in a sense of humor unmatched in other classical texts. The forger should have imitated this style as faithfully as possible and even exaggerated it a bit[10] so as to give the reader the impression that the work was indeed by al-Jahiz. The forger was doubtless the first to realize that his style was not the same as al-Jahiz's, and he may have chosen not to imitate all the nuances of his predecessor's voice. By constructing a halfhearted pastiche he may have been meaning to make it easier to claim the work later, on the assumption that it is easier to claim a disputed work than a universally accepted one.

Kitab al-mahasin wa l-addad, which depicts a variety of objects and characteristics from two opposed points of view, raises a second sort of problem. The work commences, rather distressingly, with a citation of al-Jahiz's confessions to forgery.[11] Why should a counterfeit text open with a discussion of forgery? Could the forger be using a locus classicus to disguise his own fraud by suggesting that the work is so authentic that this citation can serve as its epigram? Yet the citation is inappropriate because it has nothing to do with the subject of the book. It points to the existence of a forger who gives himself away by referring to the practices of al-Jahiz. Is this naïveté or oversophisticated second-guessing? To me, the latter seems more plausible. As soon as the work appeared, the author fell prey to "jealousy." Instead of discreetly vanishing in favor of al-Jahiz, he decided to deliberately arouse suspicion on the part of his readers. In this case, al-Jahiz has served both as pseudonym and as model. Yet his disciple declined to claim the work openly, and so failed to follow his master's example in everything. All he did was point out that he was wearing a mask. We will probably never see his real face. The mask represents al-Jahiz, but the wearer hopes not to be confused with the face he has borrowed. In fact, he hopes that someone will guess the identity that for whatever reason he is unwilling to reveal. He seems to say: "I am not who you think I am; I will not divulge my name; it is up to you to guess at the identity of my phantom body."

A further riddle comes to mind. Imagine the following situation—one that never occurred but remains a possibility. Al-Jahiz writes a book and neither claims it for himself nor credits it to someone else. Instead, he declares that a certain dead author has attributed it to *him.* He adds that the true author is unknown or, better yet, of the "older generation." When the time comes for him to claim the work, the web will be so tangled that even he will have trouble extricating himself.

Demarcations

In *Kitab al-bukhala'* (The book of misers), al-Jahiz presents himself as a transmitter reporting conversations by or about misers. For the most part, the misers themselves are real persons, not fictional characters. Al-Jahiz knew a few of them himself, and he cites them directly—that is, without a chain of authorities.

What exactly is his contribution? Did he invent the speeches he puts in the mouths of his protagonists, or is he a mere compiler of the anecdotes about misers current in his time? He certainly bears responsibility for the organization of the work, as well as for the passages where he addresses the reader directly, offers commentary, and refers to himself in the first person. Yet our question applies to the speeches attributed to the misers and the generous men—that is, the bulk of the text. Did these persons actually speak, or did they only lend their names to the enterprise? In other words, we must determine whether al-Jahiz is a tutor or a parent.

If one considers the question worthwhile at all—that is, if one decides that it matters whether the texts in the *Book of Misers* belong properly to al-Jahiz or to his protagonists—then one must adopt a method likely to result in a satisfactory answer. The only method that answers this description is the one al-Jahiz's contemporaries would have followed in the same situation. This method consists, as we know, in evaluating the chain of transmission and the reliability of the witnesses involved. Al-Jahiz himself outlines the method in one of his epistles. To test the veracity of his claims in the *Book of Misers,* it is only fair to apply the criteria he himself sets out so clearly.

For events "which one has not seen but which could have been witnessed by someone else," one can have total confidence in "accounts considered a part of common knowledge, transmitted by all and sundry persons, and familiar to everyone. Anyone who hears such accounts need not trouble to ascertain their veracity." [12] In the *Book of Misers,* it is a simple matter to isolate texts no one could accuse al-Jahiz of having invented because their authorship is a matter of universal agreement. These texts include the classical poems, proverbs, and Qur'anic verses cited in the book.

Other accounts, adds al-Jahiz, may be believed even though they are not part of the public domain. These accounts are reported by people unknown to one another and therefore incapable of having agreed among themselves to fabricate traditions. No one has ever heard of two isolated forgers producing the same text: "When a number of people have transmitted the same account, and you know that they all lived in different times and places and could not have known each other, you may safely conclude that they cannot have colluded to forge the account, no matter how obscure the account itself may be. This type of tradition cannot be counterfeit because people cannot separately concoct the same falsehood." This analysis applies to all those accounts in the *Book of Misers* that coincide with traditions reported by other authors on the authority of persons other than al-Jahiz.[13]

Here is what he has to say about the third type of tradition: "There is another type more restricted than the preceding one. This consists of accounts transmitted by one or two persons who may or may not be telling the truth. Whether you believe it or not depends on your opinion of the informant's trustworthiness *('adala).* Even so, such an account can never inspire as much confidence as accounts of the first two types." [14] This description applies to those texts, by far the most numerous, that al-Jahiz reports only on his own authority in the *Book of Misers.* We already know that al-Jahiz is untrustworthy because he habitually attributes his own writings to authors of the "older generation." Therefore we must conclude that these texts, unattested as they are by other informants, must be his own inventions.[15] In a sense, this is to his credit. He may be disqualified as a transmitter, but he appears all the more skillful a writer.

CHAPTER EIGHT

A Letter from Beyond the Grave

> The right hand takes, while the left holds.
>
> —R. Hertz, "La préeminence de la main droite, étude sur la
> polarité religieuse" in *Mélanges de sociologie religieuse et folklore*

Hand-to-Hand

Imagine someone carrying out the ritual washing of a dead body. The washer notices that one of the corpse's hands is closed. Overcome by curiosity, he resolves to pry open the dead man's fist.[1] Doing so turns out to be no easy task. The dead man balled up his fist for a reason, doubtless to conceal something. Even dead, he will not give up his secret without a struggle. The corpse washer and the corpse join battle, the one seeking knowledge and the other striving to protect the secret. Yet the outcome of the struggle is never in doubt because the washer can use both hands whereas the corpse's other hand cannot help him. The waters of purification, so to speak, eventually wear down the solid rock. The living man will exert himself upon the corpse, pry open the fist, and find whatever was hidden inside it. Stripped of his secret, the corpse will finally be buried.

What was the treasure the man entrusted to his defiant corpse? Before revealing what the washer discovered, we should note that the story could have turned out differently. The dead man's hand could have resisted so tenaciously that the washer would have had to use a tool to pry it open or call in the assistance of other living men. Or the dead man's free hand could have sprung to life suddenly and strangled the washer, dragging him into the abyss and racking up a victory for the dead over the living. We may be assured, however, that neither of these hypotheses came to pass. Indeed, we must banish them from mind altogether if we wish to remain faithful to the story, which gives us only the unambiguous victory of the washer over the corpse.

The dead man was called Ibn Naqiya. He lived in Baghdad in the eleventh century and wrote poems and riddles as well as scholarly works.[2] Classical biographical dictionaries devote only a few lines to him, and his life story appears to offer little of interest. Posterity paid scant attention to his writings, of which only a part has been preserved. Nevertheless, the modern reader feels the same fascination as the classical biographers did with Ibn Naqiya's novel way of confronting death and preparing for his meeting with God. He saw to it that death would not deprive him of the ability to communicate. He continued to live even as a powerless cadaver by addressing, to whom it may concern, a message of the utmost importance.

The Poet's Gift

Ibn Naqiya's story is reported by Ibn al-Jawzi on the authority of a transmitter who had it from the corpse washer himself: "After Ibn Naqiya's death, I went into his house to wash his corpse and found his hand closed into a fist. I exerted myself to open it, and found written inside: 'I have gone to call upon a neighbor who never disappoints his guest / Hoping to be spared the torment of Hellfire. / Despite my fear of God, I am confident / Of his bounty, for He is the most generous of benefactors.'"[3] No commentary follows this account. The story can stand on its own. Even so, it can also be explicated, that is, unfolded and pried apart,[4] finger by finger, like the dead man's hand.

If I have understood the story correctly, Ibn Naqiya scribbled two propitiatory verses on a piece of paper, folded the paper, and clutched it in his hand. Thus prepared for his journey, he waited for death, and death came. The verses were written to be read by God and by him alone. Strictly speaking, they do not form part of Ibn Naqiya's literary production because they were not published during his lifetime. They stand in the same relationship to the rest of his works as his dead body does to his living one. Reserved for God, they are not to fall into profane hands. Rather, they are to be exchanged for divine mercy by furnishing tangible proof that the dead man's last act and final thought had God and only God as their object. The verses are to follow the deceased in the afterlife, and no one is authorized to make use of them in this world, not even to edify the faithful. The closed hand is not supposed to open except in God's presence. There the paper will be unfolded and humbly offered up to the recipient who will decide, after reading it, what the sender's fate will be. Ibn Naqiya has no need to speak: half-bowed, with his eyes cast down, he has only to make the gesture of extending his arm. The communication itself will take place at a distance.

But now the message has been intercepted en route. A person other than the intended recipient has found the paper, and, busybody that he is, has repeated the story everywhere. He may even have kept the paper as a relic or as proof of the truth of the tale. No biographer bothered to ask whether the paper was put back in the dead man's hand. We will never know what the corpse washer did once he had satisfied his curiosity.

Since Ibn al-Jawzi's account has no epilogue, the reader may presume to supply one. The corpse washer has the duty, we may say, of restoring the dead man's property by putting the message back in his hand. Otherwise he will be doing a great disservice to Ibn Naqiya, who will have to present himself before God empty-handed. Salvation happens through writing. Without his ticket, Ibn Naqiya will have to explain what happened with the corpse washer and try to recite his poem by heart. Of course, this will work only if he remembers it. The Day of Judgment is supposed to be so terrifying that mothers will forget to nurse their children [Qur'an 22:2]. Without his crib sheet, Ibn Naqiya runs the risk of forgetting his Arabic and finding himself among the damned.

When should the corpse washer put the paper back? First he should finish washing and wiping down the corpse. If the paper gets wet, the writing will turn into a blot of watery ink. But after the hand dries, an unforeseen difficulty will arise: how to make the corpse take the paper back. It took a great deal of effort to pry it loose, and it will take even more effort to put it back. Another struggle ensues, this time to close the stiffened hand. Now the living must battle the dead in order to restore the latter's property. But what can the corpse washer do if the hand closes around the paper but then slackens like a loose spring and lets it drop?

In that case the washer must try again, perhaps by tying the hand closed with a bit of strong cord. All this action promises to take a long time. It is the dead man's revenge on the living. If the washer fails, he will have Ibn Naqiya's damnation on his conscience. But Ibn Naqiya, petrified with rage, stubbornly refuses to comply. What good will a crumpled piece of paper do now that his secret is out?

His plan depended on having a secret to be shared only with God. He wanted to surprise the Judge and conciliate his Lord with a demonstration of repentance entirely original and unprecedented. Because of an indiscreet corpse washer (who, moreover, never received an authorization to transmit the verse), the secret is out and the element of surprise lost.

But here I have to stop and ask whether I am mistaken in supposing that the dead man was angry. Can we be sure that Ibn Naqiya meant to address God? He could just as well have had the living in mind. When he composed his message and closed his fist around it, he must have known that it would fall into the hands of the corpse washer. In point of fact, corpse washers must wash the entire cadaver.[5] The hand, like all the limbs, must be purified by water. The washer was obliged to open the hand not out of curiosity but because his duties demand it. Ibn Naqiya must have realized that his note would not escape the vigilance of the living. Moreover, a rereading of the verses shows that they are not addressed to God directly. Ibn Naqiya may have wanted to signal his deference by referring to God in the third person. Even so, God is formally the third person, the "absent party" to the speech act.[6] The second person is the corpse washer, the very man who pried open the hand and read the message. It is true that Ibn Naqiya cannot have known his identity, but he knew that there would be someone there, and that whoever it was would open his hand and tell the tale. This outcome is probably what Ibn Naqiya wanted. The news would spread far and wide and eventually reach the ears of God himself. At this point everyone could testify in the poet's favor, and in the face of such unanimously attested repentance, God could hardly refuse to pardon his faithful servant.

We should note that the corpse washer in this case was not a professional. In all probability, he was a friend or relative of Ibn Naqiya.[7]

His name was 'Ali b. Muhammad al-Dahhan.[8] The fact that the sources give his name means that he was a known figure. From the story, he appears a worthy individual, an educated man as interested in poetry as he was in the salvation of souls, who performed the last rites for Ibn Naqiya as a pious act. If he was cited, it is because he was an authority and a man worthy of trust. As a privileged witness, he is qualified to reveal Ibn Naqiya's last confession and receive a message from beyond the grave. The first line of the message is actually in the perfect tense ("I have gone . . ."). This line is not the living man speaking, but the dead one. The message comes from the Beyond, and Ibn Naqiya was already dead when he composed it.[9]

The Birth of a Trap

So far I have spoken of Ibn Naqiya as if he had only one hand and it makes no difference whether he was holding his note in the right hand or the left. I must have been thinking for whatever reason that it was the right. I bring up the problem now only because the biographer Ibn Khallikan (thirteenth century) specifies that Ibn Naqiya's closed hand was the *left* one.[10] This detail calls my previous interpretation into question and forces me to pursue a new line of inquiry. Now it becomes necessary to find out why Ibn Naqiya chose one hand over the other. The choice of the left is disturbing: believers are called "the people of the right hand," and the wicked the ones of the left [Qur'an 56:26–43]. The left hand is sinful, unworthy, and soiled; it is the one used for tainted ablutions. The right hand is the preeminent and privileged one, explicitly ennobled by God.[11] Ibn Naqiya entrusted his left hand with the propitiatory message. We might suppose that by doing so, he acknowledges having sinned. He intends to appear before God with the humility of a sinner who makes no attempt to conceal his transgressions. But we are equally justified in saying that he should have used the other hand, the hand used for both salutation and salvation, as a way of emphasizing his repentance and showing that he numbers himself among "the people of the right hand."

Neither of these explanations is convincing. It is time for me to reveal the mistaken assumption I had in mind thus far and that led me into a blind alley. Based on a misreading of Ibn al-Jawzi and Ibn Khallikan, I assumed that the writing could have been done only on paper. I therefore placed a note in Ibn Naqiya's hand. However, nothing in either of the accounts justifies this interpretation. There is no basis for assuming that the corpse washer found a piece of paper in the dead man's hand. On the basis of what now appears to be the evidence, I can conclude only that Ibn Naqiya wrote his verses on the palm of his hand![12] Then he closed his fist to shield them from the curious corpse washer. He did not close his hand because he was afraid of losing his poem, because it was impressed upon his flesh. Rather, he did so to preserve them for God. His closed fist becomes a sheet of paper, folded and sealed; his very own body carries the inscription that records his repentance. The corpse washer has broken the seal, unrolled the fist, and seen what he should never have seen.

Ibn Khallikan also informs us that the message was scribbled and could be deciphered only with a good deal of patience. Letters were written over other letters, and the words were jumbled together. Was this because his hand was too small to fit both verses? Or because Ibn Naqiya, in his last fevered moments, could not control his handwriting? We can imagine a further possibility: by muddling his message, Ibn Naqiya was making a deliberate attempt to disguise it in such a way that only an omniscient God could make it out. However, he underestimated the intelligence of the corpse washer, who proved himself capable of unraveling the message and decoding the cryptogram. The figure of the washer now gains in interest. He not only reads well, but also possesses excellent recall: he remembers the verses after seeing them once. I do not think he would have called for paper and pen in order to write them down. He had already lost a good deal of time battling the stiffened hand and exercising his hermeneutic skills to decipher the scribbled message. The time would have come for him to finish off the task of preparing the corpse for burial.

Yet I fear his respite would have been a short one, because a new problem would necessarily have arisen. Should he wash the hand, and bear the responsibility of effacing the propitiating verses? Had Ibn Naqiya written them on a piece of paper, there would be no problem: the washer could simply replace them after washing and wiping down the hand. Yet because the verses were inscribed on the skin of the palm, washing the corpse would mean washing away Ibn Naqiya's act of contrition. It is a thorny question: the act of purification would forever efface the evidence of contrition. I can see only one way out of the dilemma. The washer must cleanse the sinning hand, and then, on the newly virgin skin, rewrite the poem. The handwriting would be different, but God in his infinite wisdom would understand and appreciate the corpse washer's complicity in conveying Ibn Naqiya's message of reconciliation and hope.

At first, it appeared inexplicable to me that Ibn Naqiya would have written his verses on his left hand. Why would he wish to greet his Lord with the impure hand? The answer is suddenly obvious: Ibn Naqiya was right-handed. He needed to use his right hand to write on his left one. Had he been left-handed, the message would have appeared on the palm of his right hand.[13]

The Prodigal Son

There is even more to the story of Ibn Naqiya's death. We must ask what it was that frightened him enough to beg for divine mercy at the moment of death. What was the sin that had to be washed away? One might think that there was nothing in particular. Believers feel doubt regarding their fate, especially in their last moments, when the hope of salvation struggles with the fear of damnation. In Ibn Naqiya's case, however, a specific fault has been recorded: he was not a firm believer. He was reproached for failing to pray, disparaging the religious law, denying resurrection,[14] and professing an interest in the foreign and therefore dangerous discipline of Greek philosophy.[15]

His biographer cites the story of the clenched fist just after an enumeration of Ibn Naqiya's errant ways. The two verses inscribed on his hand thus appear to constitute a recantation and a disavowal of his heterodox beliefs. It was certainly in Ibn Naqiya's interest to repent, but it was in the community's interest as well. Greek philosophy was an aberration, and nothing could better shore up the normative beliefs of the community than to have an errant member recant. More than personal salvation was at stake; the community's interests are involved as well. By repenting, Ibn Naqiya returns to the beliefs he had abandoned and renews his ties to his people. He did indeed transgress, but his transgression contains a lesson to anyone tempted by foreign ideas. His intellectual adventure serves as an object lesson to anyone who takes notice of it. Having repented, Ibn Naqiya rejoins the group, which emerges stronger from its confrontation with the Other. The community needs his recantation to fight off the danger he has loosed upon it and to dissuade those people who might one day seek to follow his path.

Does this mean that I question the authenticity of the story and suspect the corpse washer (or someone else) of having invented it as a way of rehabilitating a scapegoat? I have no evidence to support such a supposition, or to suggest that the corpse washer took advantage of Ibn Naqiya's demise not only to wash his body but also to whitewash his faults. Yet I may still ask whether this case is the only one of its kind. Perhaps messages from the afterlife were common currency in Ibn Naqiya's day. In other words, I must try to define the genre to which his story belongs.

The Heresiographic Dream

What do copyists dream of? Of rest, it seems. A certain copyist by the name of Ibn al-Hadina tells the following story:

> During the floods in Baghdad, my house was flooded and I lost everything. I had to do copy-work to earn a living. That year I copied out the *Sahih* of Muslim seven times. One night at the end of the year, I fell asleep and dreamed that Judgement Day had arrived. A voice called out: "Where is Ibn al-Hadina?" Then they brought me into Paradise. I lay on my back, crossed my legs, and told myself that I was through with copying. But I woke up and found my pen in my hand and the copy-sheets before me.[16]

Just as copyists dream of copying, theologians dream of theology. I am not thinking of premonitions or of visions in which God warns the dreamer to renounce the world. Rather, I mean dreams in which a theological issue is settled and salvation evoked in a heresiological dialogue with a dead person or supernatural being. Such dreams offer an opportunity to carry on a discussion with God, the Devil, the Prophet, or a noted figure recently deceased.[17] The sincerity of the dreamer matters little. Rather, the point is that such stories invoke the dead to serve the needs of the living. The moment anyone with even minor theological interest dies, some good soul will behold him in a dream and ask him about his fate in the next world. When the deceased declares that God has forgiven him, the dreamer asks why. The answer is one that might worry the historian, namely, that salvation is contingent upon certain beliefs that, as it happens, are the ones the dreamer himself professes to hold.

Like Prophetic Hadiths, dreams are trump cards in disputes between opposed schools of theological thought. Far from being erotic, dreams are a response to heresiographic necessity. The dead are not unappeasable phantoms returned to torment the living. On the contrary: they are well behaved and peaceful. From their distant posts in the afterlife, they rally around the living and take a hand in their affairs. The living invoke the dead, demand their testimony, and give them no peace until they produce the desired evidence.

Obviously, it is impossible to attribute a given speech to just any dead person. The words put in the dead man's mouth must not clash with the ones he spoke while alive, lest an unacceptable contradiction arise. Theology, in particular, cannot abide contradiction. Yet there is a way to make the dead man say something other than what he said while alive while avoiding a scandalous inconsistency. As we have seen, the solution lies in attributing a retraction, an act of repentance. The dead man has only to declare himself mistaken and admit his error. Then the dreamer can successfully attribute to him a doctrine totally at variance with the one he clung to his whole life long.

Whether the dead man's discourse matches his living one or not, the dream, vague though it may be, is final. It has only to show that the deceased was right or wrong in holding such and such an opinion. In this way, the dream guides the believers, the recipients of the dreamer's message, along the "right" path to salvation. The deceased serves as an exemplar, whether positive or negative. The dreamer recounts his dream in order to persuade his audience to embrace or reject a particular doctrine. The deceased lies with his fist clenched, and then the living open his hand, with his consent or otherwise, so they may read—or write—the meaning of his life, the phrase or two that will brand him forever.

Hand and Shroud

The two biographers mentioned thus far state that Ibn Naqiya inscribed his penitence on his hand. But a third writer throws the whole matter into confusion by stating that it was written on his shroud.[18] In that case, Ibn Naqiya must have prepared his shroud in advance by tracing his propitiatory message on the whiteness of the sheet. After his death, he was wrapped inside his own text. I cannot help wondering whether the two verses appeared in a tiny script on a corner of the shroud or in letters bold enough to fill the shroud and blacken the maximum amount of space possible. Nevertheless, I must reign in my overactive imagination in view of a sudden doubt about the correctness of this new version of the story.

In his obituary for Ibn Naqiya, the historian Ibn Kathir (fourteenth century) refers expressly to Ibn al-Jawzi, who here too uses the word *hand*. How could Ibn Kathir speak of a *shroud*, when no source mentions one? Having already made the mistake of assuming the message was written on a scrap of paper, I decided to approach this text much more cautiously. After considering the two words for a time, I realized that, astonishingly, they refer to the same thing. The Arabic word for *palm* is *kaff*, and for *shroud* it is *kafan*. The only dif-

CHAPTER NINE

Voice and Palimpsest

[Moses] said: Lord, comfort my heart, ease my task, and loosen the knot in my tongue, that they may understand my speech.

—Qur'an 10:26–29

The serpent has a forked, black tongue. Someone has claimed that serpents have two tongues, but I believe this to be an error. Rather, I think that he saw the two ends of the tongue and decided there were two separate tongues.

—Al-Jahiz, *Kitab al-hayawan*

Paper and Parchment

Writing, according to al-Jahiz, can be done on paper or on parchment. Although the meaning of the text will not change, its value will rise or fall depending on the material it is written on, just as it rises or falls depending on which author claims it (or has it attributed to him). The text's material support carries a significance of its own. Thus many dealers confess to having subjected manuscripts to procedures to make them appear older. In the paper mills established all over the Islamic empire after the end of the eighth century, manufacturers met a growing demand for "antique-looking paper . . . by treating it with saffron and fig-juice." [1]

Al-Jahiz describes writing materials in terms reminiscent of his remarks on the anecdote. An anecdote will have different effects depending on whether the subject is a buffoon or an ascetic; its success depends on the personage of whom it is told. [2] Similarly, a text will be more attractive if written on parchment than on cotton paper: "Folios of cotton-paper *(qutni)* sell cheaply in the markets, even when they contain original stories, charming witticisms, and valuable information. But if you took the same number of parchment sheets and filled them with doggerel and trivial stories, they would attract more buyers and fetch a higher price." [3]

Paper brings down the value of a text, at least in the market, whereas parchment adds value to texts that have little to recommend them in and of themselves. Paper is an evil genie that disfigures those writers who approach it, whereas parchment is a fairy godmother who confers eternal youth: "[Parchment] supports erasure and alteration more easily, and better withstands the wear and tear of borrowing and passing from hand to hand. Moreover, it retains its value and keeps its utility because you can re-use old parchments without buying new ones." [4]

Paper is fragile and comes apart under borrowing and fingering. Erasing it destroys it as well as the text. The text and the paper it is written on are so closely linked that damage to the one means damage to the other. Writing and paper are bound together in a compact of loyalty until death: neither can survive the death of the other. Paper, moreover, passes only reluctantly into the hands of a new owner. To survive, it needs a conscientious owner and reader who will handle it with loving care and, above all, refuse to lend it out and subject it to the greedy hands of borrowers. Just as paper shies away from being exchanged, it also demands a jealous partner. The exclusive relationship between the paper and the text it carries parallels the relationship between the paper and its owner. And just as the paper comes apart when anyone erases its text, it also comes apart if passed from hand to hand.

Parchment, on the other hand, behaves quite differently. It lends itself to "erasure and alteration" and, untrammeled by loyalty, chooses a wandering life of infidelity and multiple incarnations. Texts come and go, but it remains, always ready to receive new texts freely and without discrimination. Parchment enjoys complete freedom, but always carries the memory of its former texts in the form of traces, some clear and others faded, of the letters it has borne before. And for whatever obscure reason, readers still prefer parchment to paper.

The Tabooed Letter

If a text can be inseparable from the material on which it is written, the same holds true for voices as well. In certain cases, a voice takes on the properties of parchment, that is, it behaves as an auditory palimpsest by revealing a text that the speaker is trying to conceal. This event occurs most often when an individual speaks a language other than his mother tongue. With this fact in mind, we may consider the case of two personalities, one a theologian and the other a poet, who, being non-Arabs, shared an inability to pronounce the language of the Qur'an in the proper way.

The theologian Wasil b. 'Ata' (eighth century) possessed great learning, but suffered from two handicaps: his neck was too long, and he could not roll his *r*'s. The first handicap could not be cured: surgeons could hardly reduce the length of his neck to more acceptable dimensions. Wasil, who was compared to a giraffe, doubtless suffered from his deformity, particularly because he was the head of a theological sect (the prestige of whose doctrines, it seems, depended on the well-formedness of their advocate's neck). The second handicap, however, could be remedied, as in the case of the famous orator who cured his stuttering by practicing elocution with a pebble in his mouth. Al-Jahiz assures us that a month of training sufficed to cure non-Arabs of their faults in pronunciation.[5] But the unfortunate Wasil never managed to accomplish this feat, or never tried, perhaps because of some unconscious aversion to betraying his mother tongue and adopting the sounds of a foreign language. Whatever the reason for it, his failure was rendering him impotent, so he resolved to avenge himself upon the cause of his misery. I can only imagine that his lectures at the mosque (the site of theological disputations) provoked laughter in his audience, and that his many rivals had only to mimic his poorly pronounced words to ridicule the doctrine he was advocating.

One fine day, Wasil struck upon an original and unexpected solution to his problem. Unable or unwilling to correct his pronunciation, he stopped using any word containing the letter *r*. One day, then, his audience realized that one of the most common letters in Arabic no longer appeared in his speech. Try as they might, his audience could find no trace of the offending letter. Or rather, they could detect the letter, but only in the words that Wasil had avoided and replaced with others that lacked an *r*. As they followed his discourse, his readers must have noticed Wasil's continual substitution of words at every point in the syntagmatic chain. This deliberate and pitiless exhis cause. To avoid losing face before those ill-intentioned members of the audience who took less of an interest in the content of his lectures than in the possible reappearance of the letter *r*, he had to turn his every word over in his mouth before uttering it. Nevertheless, he still had to worry about those words that are so common that it was difficult if not impossible to avoid them without resorting to a paraphrase. Commenting on this predicament, al-Jahiz wonders how Wasil could manage to avoid the numbers or the names of months that contained the forbidden letter. I imagine that in the heat of disputation, his adversaries could force him to reply with a phrase that would reveal his handicap, especially because there are words that lack synonyms and that cannot be conveniently paraphrased. To avoid saying "Ramadan," he might say "the month of fasting," except that the word for *month (shahr)* contains an *r*. He would then have to resort to a further paraphrase such as "the time of fasting," an unfortunately ambiguous expression. Moving from one paraphrase to another, he would eventually make a fool of himself, which was exactly what he was trying to avoid in the first place. A forced paraphrase would reveal the artificiality of the constraint he had placed upon himself and destroy the illusion of ease he was trying to produce. The disappearance of the offending phoneme had to appear graceful, spontaneous, and, above all, natural.[8] All this activity could be carried off as long as Wasil prepared his lectures in advance. But in the midst of disputation, the futility of his efforts would surely reveal itself; the scorned letter would burst forth, stubborn and vengeful. Wasil would then have to pay the price for his presumption, and once again serve as the butt of mimicry and ridicule—even more so, for having had the temerity to take on a letter of the alphabet. Eliminating a letter from one's writing is relatively easy, but eliminating it from one's speech is a project doomed to failure. Language cannot be castrated with impunity.

The Spokesman

The second case is that of the eighth-century poet Abu 'Ata' al-Sindi. Originally from Sind, Abu 'Ata' knew Arabic perfectly, and composed good poetry in it. No one doubted his gifts, but his faulty pronunciation brought him unhappiness in an age when poetry was read aloud instead of in silence. His Arab friends, including Hammad al-Rawiya,[9] a famous transmitter of verse, would often play a malicious trick on him. In the course of conversation, they would induce him to use words he could not pronounce. To their delight, he fell for the trick every time.[10]

This kind of game is rigged from the outset. Abu 'Ata's friends knew which words he would stumble over and would fool him into saying them, meaning that their goal was to elicit a response already known to them. Shaking with suppressed laughter, they had to defer their mirth until the victim fell into the trap; then the laugh, grating and cruel, could burst out. Abu 'Ata' must have come to doubt their friendship for him, but all he could do, I imagine, is smile feebly to hide his vexation. Should he protest, he would have to do so using the very phonemes he could not pronounce, provoking renewed gales of laughter. The best response might have been for him to storm out of the room, refuse to speak with anyone again, remain fiercely silent behind closed doors, and, teeth clenched, avoid crowded places. However, he earned a living from words—that is, from poetry—so this solution would not do. Less clever than Wasil, he chose a less original solution: he asked one of his patrons to give him a slave skilled in recitation.[11] Under such conditions, the poem falls under the care of two people: the composer, who mutters it under his breath, and the reciter, who performs it out loud. In other words, the poet requires a spokesman in order to speak.[12]

Al-Jahiz remarks that one can always tell a person's origin from his pronunciation of Arabic because each ethnic group has a specific way of articulating words. One word is enough to betray one's differentness, and indeed one's animality. Authors were incapable of discussing eloquence without referring to animals (see also the Conclusion below). Furthermore, none could mention faulty pronunciation without making a joke of it or imitating it with malicious delight. Mimicry is possible only when the mimic is convinced of his superiority to the object of his imitation. Mimics, reports al-Jahiz, can imitate the barking of dogs, the braying of asses, the gestures of the blind, and the accents of non-Arabs.[13] Each of the objects of imitation suffers from a lack or deficiency: dogs and asses lack language, blind men lack sight, and non-Arabs lack the ability to produce certain sounds. By generating laughter at their expense, imitation reassures the spectator of his membership among "us," on the presumption of a complicity between the mimic and the audience and in the absence of the object, who is reduced to the status of a third person even though he appears, in the mimic's imitation, to be referring to himself.

Can an author excel in two languages? Al-Jahiz thinks not, but—as usual—contradicts himself, in this case by citing the case of a certain preacher who could expound the Qur'an in Arabic to the Arabs and in Persian to the Persians (the former sat on his right and the latter on his left).[14] I have the impression that al-Jahiz himself was monolingual, even though he sometimes mentions foreign words. Scholars have exercised themselves on the question of whether al-Jahiz knew Persian, as if the question had any importance. Al-Jahiz had no need to know another language for the simple reason that in his time, there was only one language: Arabic. The rest were only noises, a vast cacophony of howls, brays, and meows. Al-Jahiz was a happy writer: he liked to laugh, and his laughter was, up to a point, honest and without reserve.

Conclusion

Metamorphosis

What did the ancient Arabs do when they lost their way at night?
How did they recover themselves and find their way back to the
haunts of men?

You will never guess; you must concede that the cat has your
tongue; and God knows what that sensual creature will do with your
tongue now that he has it. That is another question, which I would
not know how to translate into the language of cats, but if I were you
I would keep a close watch over my tongue and protect it from the
claws of that carnivorous creature that—as you can see from his
eyes—is possessed by a demon. In any case, you must resign yourself
to listening to a discussion full of meowing and other animal noises.
How, indeed, can one speak of bilingualism without citing, evoking,
and invoking animals? Behind every articulation of language lies an
inarticulate cry. This fact is why I shall be referring in large part to the
Book of Animals by al-Jahiz, the author who owes his nickname to his
protruding eyeballs. I like to imagine that it was his contemplation of
the wonders of nature and his study of animals that made al-Jahiz's
eyes pop out. Our eyes customarily widen in astonishment; if the as-

tonishment is too great, our eyes tend to protrude, a process that I imagine might culminate in a bulging eye that never blinks.

If I seem to have lost myself in the animal kingdom, it is because my subject is one of loss, deprivation, reduction, and perdition: in sum, curiously enough, metamorphosis. Imagine a man lost in the wilderness at night. He must find his way back to his own people at any cost. He may have strewn pebbles along his path during the day, and he must have left footprints in the loose soil beneath his feet. But in the darkness of night, neither the pebbles nor the footprints are visible. The traveler doubtless possesses good eyesight: his eyes may even bulge outward, taking in more than sunken eyes can, but they are still no match for the eyes of a cat. So what can he do? As clever as a monkey, he resorts to a procedure that for all its strangeness was actually used: he begins to bark. The Arabic word *mustanbih* means just that: a man who imitates the barking of a dog.[1] As he walks along, the traveler produces random barking noises. If there are any dogs in the vicinity, they will bark back, thus revealing the location of human settlements (because dogs generally keep close to settled areas). To find his way home, the traveler must bark. To become a man (again), he must first transform himself into a dog.

Of course, the barking man is something of a trickster, as shown by how easily he deceives the dogs. Man barks by necessity, in this case because he fervently wishes to escape an unpleasant situation. The dogs, on the other hand, respond because they believe that one of their number is nearby and is addressing them in their own language. Their barking is thus the echo of a feigned barking, the echo of an echo. The call comes not from a fellow canine but from a creature of human form who under cover of darkness is pretending to be a dog. This errant mimic gains twice from the provisional renunciation of his own language and his adoption of theirs: he finds his own people, and he tricks the dogs. Necessity plays a role in this game, just as play fulfills a necessary and quite serious function. By his hypocritical mimicry, the player finds his way by passing as a dog. Later, he will have no need to bark; he will once again be able to use the language he had to suppress in order to utter the sounds of dog language.[2]

But is it certain that he will find his own people, and that his steps and his barks will lead him back to his own language?

There is no need to answer hastily, for the predicament of our unwilling nighttime traveler is very complicated. He himself may not realize how complex; he may have overestimated his power to fool the dogs. Certainly he runs a great risk by barking all alone in the darkness of the night. What if, upon reaching a settlement, he finds he has lost his tongue? What if, in response to questions, he can only bark? What if he can no longer use the language of his family, the language he learned from the cradle or even earlier, the language he learned to speak by watching and imitating the movements of his mother's lips? This possibility cannot be excluded, no matter how unlikely it may seem. Night is a magical time, full of evil spells and enchantments. It would not surprise me if by some mysterious process a lost traveler were transformed into a dog, or if a barking man were to lose sight of the game and begin barking in earnest. Imitation has its price: think of all the game players who have come to deadly blows. Mimicking another is a dangerous game, for one plays with shadows, and shadows may solidify; so too may barking cause one to forget articulate language. Imagine a man imitating a dog for a time, then deciding that enough is enough and it is time to stop playing and become serious. He decides to stop barking, but to his dismay, he cannot find the words he has always been able to pronounce. He concentrates, coughs, takes a deep breath, and clears his throat, all to no avail: the only sounds coming from his mouth are barks.

Dogs and Men

How will the traveler's people react? His predicament will strike them as strange and totally unforeseen. The myths and stories current in the tribe say nothing about a man who one fine day just started barking. Disconsolate, though saying among themselves that they might do better to laugh, relatives and friends surround the lost child and bemoan his fate. Eventually, however, irritation gets the better of compassion. They do not disown him, certainly, for he is still one of their own. Up to a point, they sympathize with his sufferings, and they vow in great earnest never to abandon him. Yet their unease grows and inexorably becomes the sole subject of conversation, conversation that now has the added attraction of furnishing everyone with an opportunity to prove to themselves and each other that they can speak and not bark.

Our unfortunate hero begins to display worrisome symptoms. He can no longer abide cats, he enjoys gnawing on bones, and he favors the company of dogs. He understands everything that is said to him or to anyone else, but because he cannot express himself except by barking, he learns to vary his barks. Depending on the situation, he howls, squeals, yelps, yaps, or bays. When his tribesmen debate a serious issue, he formulates his opinion in a disturbing and incongruous series of yelps. Of his fellow men, the medicine man is probably the most vexed of all, because his charms and exorcisms have done nothing to expel the canine demon. Unwilling to compromise his prestige by admitting failure, he points an accusing figure at our hero and announces that he is an impostor with evil designs against the community. This charge fails to persuade the people, so the medicine man turns on the skeptics and accuses them of having succumbed to canine influences. To forestall civil unrest, a compromise is reached: the barker will not be put to death or chased from the settlement, but instead will have his mouth (or muzzle?) forced shut whenever a solemn ceremony is taking place. Two men will hold his head in a firm grip, as if in a vice, and thus prevent him from yelping.

But these statements are all speculation. Perhaps I should cease playing with words and with barkings, stop tracking the night traveler, and abandon the canine metaphor. I should doubtless drop the thread of a discourse that threatens to subdivide into infinite permutations. Yet I cannot just abandon the *mustanbih* to his lonely wanderings in the night. I must find out what happens to him, and thus find an ending to our story.

To continue, then: Dogs guide lost men to human settlements. The traveler has only to set off calmly toward the dogs, guided by the sound of their barking. But I may be too optimistic when I say that he will find his own people again. Dogs are everywhere; the ones he is following may not be his own. Because so much depends on the workings of chance, we must admit the possibility of strange dogs. My own hopes for the traveler do not count: his march has a logic of its own, and I can do nothing for him. All I can do is try to foresee the different paths that lay open before him, and before the progress of my story.

At first glance (albeit we are in the middle of the night), there are only two possible outcomes. Either the traveler will find his tribe or he will find himself among strangers. But then again, there are other epilogues, each a beginning in itself. Here is a possibility you have not imagined: the dogs that respond to the traveler's bark are not dogs at all, but other men who are lost and who are themselves barking to find their way home. In that case, a double deception is taking place: both sides are false dogs believing themselves to be dealing with real ones. At a certain point, the two sides will meet, everyone will be disappointed, and the quest must begin all over again.

Then again, even if the dogs that respond to the barking of men are real dogs, there is no guarantee that a human settlement is actually nearby. The dogs may be lost—and dogs do lose their way sometimes, despite their homing instincts and heightened senses. Obviously they make mistakes, such as taking a feigned bark for a real one, or a man for a dog. Real dogs, false dogs, and other narrative possibilities all beckon to me now, but I shall leave them hanging for a moment, for I have other fish to fry, and there is more than one way to skin a cat.[3]

Back, then, to our traveler. When he hears dogs barking in the distance, he decides that two possible outcomes exist. Either he will find his own people or he will find a group of strangers. Dogs, unfortunately, are monolingual, and familiar dogs bark the same way foreign ones do. At night, all dogs bark alike. I shall indulge the traveler's optimism and let him wend his way home. Yet I know that he will find no peace. A nasty shock awaits him: his heart beating, he approaches his people, only to find that instead of speaking their usual language, they are barking. What happened was this: in their eagerness to find their lost kinsman, they all took to barking as a way of signaling their presence to him. Having reached the village, the traveler is greeted with barks disguised as words of welcome. The fate that could or should have befallen him has now befallen his tribe.

Unless, of course, it is the whole village that has lost its way in the night and is wandering in search of its campfires, campfires that still burn somewhere, as uselessly as the stars, and in search of its language, once so unthinkingly squandered, leaving only the futile sound of barking.

Wanderings

The home fires are still burning, and it is perhaps their reflection one can see in the sky. The tribe has deserted the camp to go in search of their lost kinsman and their lost language. They wander, barking all the way, and one day they will have to scan the skies for some sign of where their camp might be. For the camp is lost now too or—what amounts to the same thing—has fallen into the hands of foreigners. Meanwhile the traveler hurries on his way, thinking he has found his goal at last. The dogs are barking, and the campfires glow just around the bend. But, as you will have guessed, he will find no welcome there. His friends and family have departed, and the people he finds in their place will display no eagerness to see him. Indeed, they will quickly extinguish the fires in hopes of turning away their unwelcome guest.

I must pause a moment to prepare you for what happens next. The word *mustanbih,* our point of departure, has connotations not only of wandering and soliciting the barking of dogs, but also of the search for a hospitable campfire. Barking alone cannot serve to indicate where the settlement lies, because dogs, as we have seen, may be mistaken. Rather, it serves to guide the traveler toward a second and unmistakable sign: the flame and smoke of the hearth. If the people who lie at the end of the traveler's path wish to deny him hospitality, they extinguish their fires. Not with water, but with urine: as a famous line of poetry has it, "They ask their mother to piss on the fire."[4] She places herself across the hearth and releases a stream of urine—a thin stream, no doubt, because being a miser and a mother of misers, she hesitates to let go of anything. The poet does not relate whether this meager liquid suffices to put out the flames, although the flames are probably faint enough already: a tribe that retains its urine will hardly heap wood freely on its fires. In any case, the traveler will find no welcome. I advise him to escape as quickly as possible, for he runs the risk of being devoured by the starving dogs that roam the campsites of the misers.[5]

Should the traveler instead find himself among a generous tribe of strangers, he will have a different but equally disappointing experience. In the generous village, there are also dogs roving about, but as another poet says by way of compliment, they are cowardly dogs who do not bark.[6] So many guests come and go that the dogs, submerged in a continual flood of two-legged visitors seeking food and lodging, have lost their bearings. So often do their masters command them to behave that they have lost the habit of barking. Instead they spend their time eating the copious leftovers the guests toss away. They become as welcoming as their masters, albeit for reasons of their own. Yet this idyllic picture leaves me unsatisfied. Dogs who no longer bark, dogs condemned to silence, dogs who open their jaws only to eat— are they still dogs? I would like to acknowledge the generosity of their masters, but how am I to find the tribe in the first place if the dogs do not bark to lead me to the camp as I wander lost in the night? I suspect that this tribe is even less hospitable than the misers, who after all never muzzled their dogs. Admittedly they extinguish their fires, but I can still feel their presence, and their presence comforts me. I know that people are out there somewhere, and, willingly or not, they are communicating with me through the mediation of their dogs. With people whose dogs have forgotten how to bark, communication is impossible. No sound guides me to their camp, and even as I tell myself that it lies only a short distance away, every step carries me in the opposite direction. I can bark all I want, but no one will answer me.

Aping

Let us nevertheless imagine that our traveler eventually glimpses the campfires of a foreign tribe, that the tribe speaks a human language, and that the traveler, once arrived, recovers his own tongue. What happens now? Whatever he does, the traveler will appear to be an animal. When two languages live side by side, one or the other will always appear bestial.[7] If you do not speak as I do, you are an animal. The "I" in this case must occupy the dominant position; if I am the weaker party, it is I who am the animal. To call this situation a conflict is incorrect, because a conflict requires adversaries of equal or at least comparable strength. A lion may battle a tiger, but he simply devours a rabbit. Bilingualism does not invoke an image of two gladiators advancing upon each other armed with nets and tridents; rather, it suggests that one of the two combatants is already sprawled in the dust awaiting the fatal blow (the Caesars of the Roman annals never spare the life of a fallen gladiator).

Our hero will soon discover this fact for himself. His path has carried him among people whose language he does not speak and who, for that reason, consider him an animal. He is not a dog, for he stopped barking when he found them, but rather a monkey. This monkey does not imitate the language of dogs, but the barking of men. Yet he has no illusions about his own condition. Every attempt to speak requires earnest effort, whereas his hosts speak as easily and as comfortably as they breathe. The effort makes him a monkey and singles him out as a mimic, because imitation requires effort. In other words: the monkey—that is, our traveler of a moment ago—seeks to rid himself of his simian nature in order to resemble his interlocutors, who are human beings. Being inferior to his betters, who regard him with a combination of curiosity and unease, he must resort to mimicry. He mimics precisely because he is other than the object of his mimicry; he mimics that which he cannot succeed in being, and he knows it. The others know it too: unlike the dogs, who let themselves be taken in by the mimic, they will realize that imitation cannot make a man. Herein is the paradox of imitation: one wants to be "like," but when all is said and done, one has only proved one's difference. One cannot reproduce what one is not, and likeness can never be identity. Imitation lives in the space between being and seeming, and no matter how well executed, it can never abolish difference.

On the other side of the mirror, the mimic's audience finds itself in an enviable position. They have nothing to hide because "being" and "seeming" for them are one and the same. They display themselves in the full light of day, under a noonday sun that casts no shadows. As for the monkey, he is a born hypocrite. He is always hiding something, and a long shadow extends unacknowledged behind him. Once lost in the night, now he is lost among strangers, his fellow human beings. Being an imitator, he is also necessarily a liar.

Sometimes, just to amuse themselves, the spectators give in to the enticements of mimicry. After all, monkeys are amusing creatures, and no one can resist the urge to mimic a mimic. So in their free moments, they imitate the monkey. They are not trying to be the monkey, but to be like him. Now the likeness of the monkey is an image of themselves, because it is they whom the monkey is trying to resemble. In aping the monkey's grimaces, they are imitating themselves. It is a deformed image of themselves, but their own nonetheless.

As I write these lines, I feel an uneasiness I cannot quell. What if speaking about animals turns me into one? What if, as I write of dogs, I suddenly become a dog, and lose my language (or more precisely, my languages) and suddenly start barking? I console myself with the thought that no one is safe from the canine demon. The reader may well open his or her mouth and, instead of the usual morphemes and phonemes, expel only a monotonous sort of bark. If it worries you, clap a hand over your mouth, grit your teeth, and think about something else.

What has happened, meanwhile, to our traveler? He labors on, barking as he goes. He may be in a deserted wilderness, abandoned even by the dogs (for there are places even dogs will not go). If so, he can bark all night without receiving an answer.

But the night will end, and, with the first rays of dawn, all the dogs in creation will cease to bark, as if by magic. The traveler reaches a stream and stoops to drink. As he does so, he sees his image in the clear, cool water. What does he look like? A dog? No, that outcome would be too easy. Besides, we would have to decide what breed of dog he sees reflected in the water, and the choice might prove onerous. Rather, we must say that the traveler sees his own familiar image reflected in the water. Reunited with himself, he breathes a sigh of relief. The terrors of the night have not destroyed him; he has emerged in one piece from the trial of shadows.

But he is wrong. I know this is true, and he will soon realize it as well. The water flows, and the image dances gaily atop the ripples. Suddenly, it moves sideways, and the current carries it off. Thunderstruck, the traveler gazes in the water just below him, but cannot find himself anywhere. The image has disappeared forever.

Notes
References

Notes

Introduction

1. "In literary matters, too, the dominant notion [among the Tlönians] is that everything is the work of one single author. Books are rarely signed. The concept of plagiarism does not exist; it has been established that all books are the work of one single writer, who is timeless and anonymous" (Jorge Luis Borges, "Tlön, Uqbar, Orbis Tertius," 28).

2. One should distinguish here between an author who has written only one book and an author who has written several. In the former case, the author's name opens no "horizon of expectations"; in the second, it evokes the familiar. In this connection, P. Lejeune has noted: "Perhaps one is not a true author until one has written a second book, at which point the proper name printed on the cover becomes the 'common denominator' of at least two different texts and thus gives the idea of a person who cannot be reduced to one or the other of the texts and, because capable of producing more works, transcends them all" *(Le Pacte autobiographique,* 23). [*On Autobiography,* 11.]

3. This characteristic applies to cultures besides the Arab one. Speaking of French classicism, G. Genette has remarked: "In the poetic consciousness of classicism, every individual stylistic peculiarity, almost as soon as it was noticed, was interpreted or converted, and thus reabsorbed, as a generic and timeless feature" *(Palimpsestes,* 97).

4. *Republic* 393A-C; English translation in Plato, *The Republic,* translated by Paul Shorey, 225–29. Cf. G. Genette, *Figures II,* 50–56; R. Dupont-Roc, "Mimesis et énonciation," 6–14.

5. "Poetry is not the people's assembly, where everyone speaks in turn and

under his own name. The poet is alone and speech is exclusively his, for he has no one to whom to address it" (J. Lallot, "La Mimesis selon Aristote et l'excellence d'Homère," 15).

6. To summarize: an author can assume a discourse, that is, he can speak in his own name; he can also report a discourse, as in the case of citation; and finally, he can attribute a discourse to a historical or fictional character. Broadly speaking, these three activities may be reduced to two:

(a) assumed discourse
(b) reported discourse
—unattributed
—attributed
—exactly
—falsely
—fraudulently
—fictively

When the speaker's voice merges with the culture's, it is often difficult to establish the origin of the utterance with any precision. On this diffuse, collective, and anonymous sort of discourse, see R. Barthes, *S/Z*, 48 [*S/Z*, translated by Richard Miller, 41]; D. Sperber, *Le Savoir des anthropologues*, 76–79.

7. J. M. Lotman and A. Pjatigorskij, "Le Texte et la fonction," 207.

8. Cf. M. Arkoun, *Contribution à l'étude de l'humanisme arabe au IVᵉ/Xᵉ siècle*, 148–49. On the notion of *auctoritas* in medieval theological discourse, see A. Compagnon, *La Seconde Main*, 218–21.

9. I express my gratitude to Joseph van Ess, Brigitte Foulon, Bernard Meyer, and Jean-Claude Berchet for their help in the course of writing this book.

1. Verses and Reverses

1. Al-Zawzani, *Sharh al-mu'allaqat al-'ashr*, 234; English translation in Michael Sells, *Desert Tracings: Six Classic Arabian Odes*, 48.

2. This theme is often associated with tears, as in the *mu'allaqa* of Imru' l-Qays: "Stop and let us weep at the memory of a beloved and a camp at the edge of the curling dune, between al-Dakhul and Hawmal . . . / Where my companions have stopped their mounts, saying: 'Perish not of sorrow, and be brave!' / My remedy lies in shed-

ding tears, for none can comfort me as I stand beside the vanished camp" (Al-Zawzani, *Sharh al-mu'allaqat al-'ashr,* 29, 32–33).

3. B. Tomachevski, "Thématique," 300–301.

4. Cf. H. Bloom, *The Anxiety of Influence.*

5. Ibn Rashiq, *Al-'Umda,* 1:74.

6. Ibid.

7. Khaula is the name of the beloved. Al-Zawzani, *Sharh al-mu'allaqat al-'ashr,* 91; English translation in A. J. Arberry, *The Seven Odes: The First Chapter in Arabic Literature,* 83.

8. Al-Zawzani, *Sharh al-mu'allaqat al-'ashr,* 159; Sells, *Desert Tracings,* 35.

9. Al-Zawzani, *Sharh al-mu'allaqat al-'ashr,* 162; Sells, *Desert Tracings,* 35.

10. Ibn Manzur, *Akhbar Abi Nuwas,* 55; cited in A. Trabulsi, *La Critique poétique des Arabes jusqu'au Ve siècle de l'hégire,* 114–15.

11. A classical orator tells of an initiation similar to that of Abu Nuwas: "My father made me memorize a thousand sermons and then said, 'Pretend to have forgotten them *(tanasaha).*' So I did, and speechmaking came easily to me after that" (cited in Ibn Tabataba, *'Iyar al-shi'r,* 10). What can it possibly mean to "pretend to forget"?

12. Ibid., 78, 10.

2. Adoption

1. Ibn Rashiq, *'Umda,* 2:265.

2. Cf. D. Likhatchev, "L'Étiquette littéraire"; and P. Zumthor, *Essai de poétique médiévale,* 117–20.

3. On *sariqat,* see Trabulsi, *Critique,* 192–213; G. E. von Grunebaum, *Kritik und Dichtkunst,* 101–29; and W. Heinrichs, *Arabische Dictung und griechische Poetik,* 82–99. For interesting remarks on the notion of literary property in antiquity, see H. Peter, *Wahrheit und Kunst, Geschichtsschreibung und Plagiat im Klassichen Altertum*; and E. Stemplinger, *Das Plagiat in der griecheschen Literatur.*

4. Ibn Rashiq, *'Umda,* 2:277; al-Qazwini, *Al-Idah fi 'ulum al-balagha,* 575–90.

5. On *versification* and *prosification,* see Genette, *Palimpsestes,* 244–53.

6. Ibn Rashiq, *'Umda,* 2:274–75, 265.

7. On their universality, see Al-Jurjani, *Asrar al-balagha,* 219.

8. Cf. T. Todorov, *Symbolisme et interprétation,* 77.

9. Al-Jurjani, *Asrar al-balagha,* 274.

10. Ibn Rashiq, *'Umda,* 1:235.
11. The poet is described as *abu 'udhrihi,* "the taker of [the idea's] virginity."
12. Ibn Rashiq, *'Umda,* 1:173.
13. Ibid., 2:277.
14. Al-Jurjani, *Asrar al-balagha,* 219.
15. Ibn Rashiq, *'Umda,* 2:269.
16. Ibid.
17. Ibid.
18. Ibid., 270–71.
19. Al-Jahiz, *Kitab al-bayan wa l-tabyin,* 2:228–29.

3. The Polyandrous Ode

1. Ibn Rashiq, *'Umda,* 2:136.
2. It is a different matter, of course, when the portrait is a stylized depiction of a human type, and is therefore generalized from the outset.
3. It would appear difficult to paint a portrait in which two persons recognize themselves. How could a sitter recognize herself as well as someone else in the same portrait? One might imagine that a painter of the apostles who uses his own face as a model for Saint Peter's has given two persons the same face. But it is only because the apostle has no face. Were Saint Peter to view the painting, he would recognize, at best, only his keys.
4. Qudama b. Ja'far, *Naqd al-Shi'r,* 88–101.
5. Ibn Rashiq, *'Umda,* 2:123.
6. A historian notes that "a veritable 'hierarchy of costume' stipulated, for every member of the social pyramid, the dress appropriate to his rank. As in Byzantium during the same period, to wear a fabric or ornament reserved for the sovereign constituted a crime of lèse-majesté. To wear fabric of a quality permitted by custom only to one of a higher rank was to be guilty of an offense comparable to the modern crime of wearing wrongful insignia" (M. Lombard, *Les Textiles dans le monde musulman,* 179).
7. Ibn Rashiq, *'Umda,* 2:109.
8. Ibid., 136. On self-plagiarism, or more exactly self-citation *(Selbstzitate),* see Stemplinger, *Plagiat,* 185–93.
9. Ibn Rashiq, *'Umda,* 2:136.

10. Ibid.

11. Qudama b. Ja'far, *Naqd al-Shi'r*, 111.

4. The Paths of the Prophetic Hadith

1. Ibn al-Jawzi, *Kitab al-mawdu'at*, 1:42. On Hadith, see I. Goldziher, *Muslim Studies; Encyclopedia of Islam, New Edition,* s.v. "Hadith"; J. van Ess, "L'Autorité de la tradition prophétique dans la théologie mu'tazilite" [and G. H. A. Juynboll, *Muslim Tradition: Studies in Chronology, Provenance, and Authorship of Early Hadith*].

2. Al-Amidi, *Al-Ihkam fi usul al-ahkam*, 2:103, 101.

3. Cf. Nur al-Din 'Atr, *Manhaj al-naqd fi 'ulum al-Hadith,* 83–84.

4. Al-Amidi, *Al-Ihkam fi usul al-ahkam*, 2:109. Equally unacceptable are those people who abandon God's teachings and live in chaos and dissipation (103).

5. Cf. 'Atr, *Manhaj,* 86.

6. Ibn Qutayba, *Ta'wil mukhtalif al-Hadith;* French translation in G. Lecomte, *Le Traité des divergences du "hadith,"* 86.

7. Goldziher, *Muslim Studies,* 2:134.

8. Ibid., 136.

9. Ibn al-Jawzi, *Kitab al-mawdu'at,* 1:37–46.

10. Ibn al-Jawzi states: "I forbid the reader to recite a Hadith out of my book without including the denunciation that goes along with it; otherwise he will be violating the Law" (ibid., 52).

11. Ibid., 105, 106, 81. "This Hadith is obviously false; no Muslim could fabricate such a thing. It is an utterly flimsy and contrived forgery, it being impossible because the Creator does not create himself" (ibid., 105).

12. Ibid., 48, 49, 245.

13. Ibid., 49–50.

5. Poetry and Coin

1. J.-J. Schmidt, *Les "Mou'allaqat," poésie arabe préislamique;* J. Berque, *Les Dix Grandes Odes arabes de l'Anté-Islam.* [English translations of the *mu'allaqat* include Arberry, *Seven Odes;* and Sells, *Desert Tracings,* which includes excellent modern translations of three of the odes.]

2. R. Blachère, *Histoire de la littérature arabe,* 1:174.

3. Ibid., 177–78 ("pastiche" here meaning "forgery").

4. Ibid., 157.

5. On these questions see Taha Husayn, *Fi l-adab al-jahili.* Also noteworthy is the borrowing of identities and the mischievous pleasure of fooling one's audience. Often poets would recite a poem on the understanding that it had been composed by one of their predecessors. When the audience expressed admiration, the poet would claim the poem as his own. Doing so places the audience in the awkward position of acknowledging his talent, though the poet runs the risk of being rebuked for his falsehood, especially if the trick changes the audience's opinion of the poem.

6. Blachère, *Histoire,* 1:118.

7. Al-Jumahi, *Tabaqat fuhul al-shu'ara',* 1:7.

8. Pre-Islamic poetry resembles anonymous works such as the *Thousand and One Nights* that have thrived despite the absence of authors to certify them. It is nevertheless true that the Arabs have historically held the *Nights* in low esteem. Modern efforts to find the sources of the *Nights* (Indian, Persian, Greek) accentuate the problem of the author. For lack of named authors, scholars attempt to determine which cultures contributed to the elaboration of the stories. Nothing is more troubling than a work of unknown provenance. Caspar Hauser, for instance, continues to fascinate genealogists.

9. Berque, *Dix Grandes Odes,* 44, 43.

10. When a painting thought to be the work of a master is revealed as a forgery, it loses its market value and becomes an embarrassment. No matter how skilled the forgery, neither museums nor collectors will have anything to do with it. Nevertheless, I have been told (though I have not checked) that there exists somewhere in Europe a museum containing only forged Vermeers.

6. The Poetics of the Anecdote

1. Al-Jahiz, *Kitab al-hayawan,* 4:50.

2. On this author see *Encyclopedia of Islam, New Edition,* s.v. "Djâhiz"; C. Pellat, *Le Milieu basrien et la Formation de Djâhiz.*

3. Al-Baghdadi, *Al-Farq bayn al-firaq,* 163.

4. See, for example, Hasan al-Sandubi, *Adab al-Jahiz,* 2.

5. Cf. Pellat, *Milieu,* 57.

6. "Like him!" *(mithl hadha!)*. The "like" indicates not identity but resemblance—either between al-Jahiz and the Devil, or between him and the image of the Devil that is to be carved. On the other hand, there is also a case for identity: had the woman brought the Devil himself into the shop, she would certainly have said "Like him!"

7. Ibn Rashiq, *'Umda*, 2:116.

8. Ibid.

9. It bears repeating that behind the poem's explicit addressee (the beloved), there is a second, implicit one: the lover of poetry, often the same person as the critic. It is this level of communication that concerns the theorist of poetry, because it is the forum where the poet displays his mastery of the medium.

10. Qudama b. Ja'far, *Naqd al-shi'r*, 146.

11. Ibn Rashiq, *'Umda*, 2:118.

12. Ibid.

13. Cf. Taha Husayn, *Hadith al-arbi'a*, 207.

14. Al-Jahiz, *Kitab al-bukhala'*, 8. French translation by Charles Pellat, *Le Livre des avares*. [English translation of selections in *The Life and Works of Jahiz*, 236–53.]

15. Ibid., 7.

16. Ibid.

17. Ibid., 158.

18. Cf. Barthes, *S/Z*, p. 74–75 [*S/Z*, translated by Miller, 58].

19. Al-Jahiz, *Kitab al-bukhala'*, 40.

20. Ibid., 7.

21. Ibid., 7–8.

22. "The same remark will seem freedom of speech in one's mouth, madness in another's, and arrogance in a third" (Quintilian, *The Institutio oratoria of Quintilian*, 175). F. Ast has remarked: "The meaning of a work and of any one of its passages *(Stelle)* emerges from the mind and inclinations of its author. Only a reader who has grasped these elements is qualified to understand each passage in the light of his familiarity with the author's mind. For example, a passage by Plato will often have a different meaning than a passage by, say, Aristotle, even though in both cases the words and the sense may be similar. . . . Not only the same word but indeed the same segment of text will have a different meaning based on their respective contexts" (cited in Todorov, *Symbolisme and interprétation*, 151 n. 1). [*Symbolism and Interpretation*, 157 n. 6.]

23. In al-Jahiz's time, the importance of proper attribution applied not only in literature but in medicine as well. Physicians, he says, had to be Christians. There were some Muslim physicians, but they could barely make a living, even during epidemics. One such practitioner, a "knowledgeable, patient, solicitous, and well-spoken man," was asked the reason for his lack of business. "First of all, people know I am a Muslim, and even before I began practicing, and indeed before I was even born, they decided that Muslims never succeed in medicine. Second, my name is Asad, whereas I should have been named Salib ('cross'), Gabriel, or John" (al-Jahiz, *Kitab al-bukhala'*, 102).

7. Confessions of a Forger

1. Al-Jahiz, "Kitab fasl ma bayn al-'adawa wa l-hasad," 1:350; cf. also the French translation, "De la différence entre l'hostilité et l'envie," in *Quatre Essais*.

2. Books were studied for the purpose of transmitting them. Aspiring transmitters often undertook long journeys in order to meet authors and receive their authorization, which could apply to a single work or to a whole oeuvre. See Goldziher, *Muslim Studies*, 2:168–80.

3. Al-Jahiz, *Rasa'il*, 1:350. Writers earned their keep by dedicating their works to princes who would protect and reward them. The prince, possessed of "the power to advance a career or retard it, to elevate a man or bring him low, and to compel obedience with promises and threats," lived in an atmosphere of jealousy and intrigue (ibid.). Writers had therefore to possess not only literary talent but also an aptitude for conspiracy.

4. Ibid., 351.

5. "So long as they transmit accounts on the authority of their predecessors and pass on the legacy of their elders, they may be credited with faithful guardianship of their trust but not with originality" *(fadilat man istanbat)* (ibid., 96).

6. Ibid., 351.

7. Or in the words of M. Nadeau: "One cannot simply claim to be a forger; one must also prove it" (cf. Genette, *Palimpsestes*, 178–79).

8. The most frustrated parties here would be the transmitters, who must suddenly revise their accounts of how al-Jahiz's works were transmitted, or perhaps his rivals, who cannot bear to see him triumph as both transmitter and author. It makes sense for him to have waited until he became successful before putting forth his claims of authorship (cf. Pellat, *Milieu*, 139).

9. See Pellat's introduction to his translation of *Kitab al-taj*, translated as *Livre de la couronne*, 11–13.

10. See Genette, *Palimpsestes*, 96.

11. See Pellat, *Milieu*, 139.

12. Al-Jahiz, "Al-ma'ash wa l-ma'ad," 1:119.

13. Ibid. Of course, it applies only if the authors had no contact with al-Jahiz.

14. Al-Jahiz, *Rasa'il*, 1:120.

15. Or at least that a large portion of them are.

8. A Letter from Beyond the Grave

1. Nothing fascinates the hero of a story as much as a closed door he is forbidden to open. He knows that on the other side of the door something lies revealed, and its concealment is a mystery he cannot control. After some hesitation, he invariably opens the door, and the adventure begins.

2. See C. Huart, "Les séances d'Ibn Nâqiyâ," 437–42; *Encyclopedia of Islam, New Edition*, s.v. "Ibn Nâkiyâ."

3. Ibn al-Jawzi, *Al-Muntazam fi ta'rikh al-muluk wa l-umam*, 9:69.

4. See Barthes, *S/Z*, 82–83. [*S/Z*, translated by Miller, 88–89.]

5. On the funerary rites described in ancient Arabic texts see I. Grütter, "Arabische Bestattungsbraüche in frühislamischer Zeit."

6. See E. Benveniste, "Structure des relations de personne dans le verbe," 288.

7. Preparing a body for burial was considered a pious act (see Grütter, "Arabische Bestattungsbraüche," 162ff). A historian cites the case of a man who prepared ten thousand corpses for burial; at the rate of one per day, it would have taken thirty years (Ibn Kathir, *Al-Bidaya wa l-nihaya*, 12:19). Before dying, some people designated the person whom they wished to prepare their corpses (3:119).

8. Ibn al-Jawzi, *Al-Muntazam fi ta'rikh al-muluk wa l-umam*, 9:69.

9. Or, less provocatively: he wrote the poem before he died, but he speaks in the poem as if already dead. In his discussion of an analogous case, R. Barthes remarks that "in the totality of all possible linguistic combinations, the collocation of the first person ('I') with the attribute 'dead' is precisely the one that is radically impossible. This is the unfilled place or blind spot of language" (Barthes, "Analyse textuelle d'un conte d'Edgar Poe," 48). To accomplish this feat, of course, Ibn Naqiya had only to substi-

tute the perfect tense ("I have gone") for the present ("I am going"). See Fontanier, *Les Figures du discours,* 293.

10. "It is said that the man who carried out the washing of [Ibn Naqiya's] corpse found the left hand closed. With some effort, he opened it, and found there lines written one atop another. He examined this writing and was able to read it, and it said . . ." (Ibn Khallikan, *Wafayat al-a'yan,* 3:99).

11. See al-Jurjani, *Asrar al-balagha,* 288.

12. Several colleagues to whom I showed the Arabic text misunderstood it in the same way I did. Clearly, writing on one's palms was an unusual practice.

13. Ibn Muqla, one of the great Arabic calligraphers, had his right hand cut off. Unwilling to abandon his art, he had his pen attached to the stump and continued to practice calligraphy. See A. Khatibi and M. Sijelmassi, *L'Art calligraphique arabe,* 135. He did not even think of trying to write with his left hand, which I imagine would have been more comfortable. As it happens, they later cut out his tongue.

14. Ibn al-Jawzi, *Al-Muntazam fi ta'rikh al-muluk wa l-umam,* 9:69.

15. Ibn Khallikan, *Wafayat al-a'yan,* 3:99.

16. Ibn Kathir, *Al-Bidaya wa l-nihaya,* 12:153.

17. Ibid., 24, 88, 117, 141, 145, passim.

18. "Someone related that he had found written in [Ibn Naqiya's] shroud the following lines . . ." (ibid., 141).

9. Voice and Palimpsest

1. Lombard, *Textiles,* 203, 206.

2. See also above, p. 000.

3. Al-Jahiz, "Risala fi l-hazl wa l-jidd," 2:253.

4. Ibid.

5. Al-Jahiz, *Kitab al-bayan wa l-tabyin,* 1:16, 36.

6. Ibid., 15, 16–17.

7. In G. Perec's lipogrammatic novel *La Disparition,* the letter *e* is conspicuous by its absence (if one is warned that the author never uses it). [Astonishingly, the work has been translated into English by Gilbert Adair as *A Void;* see also James Thurber, *The Wonderful O.*] See also Todorov, *Les Genres du discours,* 302 [English translation in *Genres in Discourse,* 122]; Genette, *Palimpsestes,* 49.

8. Al-Jahiz, *Kitab al-bayan wa l-tabyin,* 1:22, 16.

9. A famous falsifier, Hammad was also false to his friend 'Ata.'

10. Ibn Qutayba, *Kitab al-shi'r wa l-shu'ara'*, 2:652–53.

11. See J. Fück, *'Arabiya*, 30.

12. The poet's muteness resembles the deafness of the famous musician who conducted his compositions without being able to hear the orchestra: in fact, he was directing only his own inner music, for the orchestra was actually following the direction of a second *chef d'orchestre* who was hidden from public view.

13. Al-Jahiz, *Kitab al-bayan wa l-tabyin*, 1:69–70.

14. Al-Jahiz, *Kitab al-hayawan*, 1:76–77; al-Jahiz, *Kitab al-bayan wa l-tabyin*, 1:368.

Conclusion

1. Or as al-Jahiz defines it, a man "who howls so dogs will reply" *(Kitab al-hayawan*, 1:379).

2. Does a dog, I wonder, need a tongue in order to bark? Is it as necessary to him as it is to a human being?

3. Only figuratively, of course.

4. The line is by al-Akhtal: "Qawmun idha stanbaha l-adyafu kalbahumu / qalu li-ummihim buli 'ala n-nari" ("A people who, when guests bark for them, / say to their mother 'Piss on the fire!'") (al-Jahiz, *(Kitab al-hayawan*, 1:384).

5. The dogs may even be rabid. Al-Jahiz notes that a person bitten by a rabid dog will bark (ibid., 2:10–11).

6. The line is by Ibn Harama: "Ana jabanu l-kalbi mahzulu l-fasil" ("My dog is cowardly and my camel thin") (al-Jurjani, *Dala'il al-i'jaz*, 263).

7. Compare, for example, Columbus's attitude toward the inhabitants of the New World (T. Todorov, *La Conquête de l'Amérique*, 36–37, 54). [English translation in *The Conquest of America*, 30–32, 48.]

References

Note: The article "al-" in names and titles is disregarded in alphabetization.

Classical Works

Al-Amidi. *Al-Ihkam fi usul al-ahkam*. 4 vols. Beirut: Dar al-kutub al-'ilmiya, 1980.

Al-Baghdadi. *Al-Farq bayn al-firaq*. Beirut: Dar al-Afaq al-Jadida, 1973.

Al-Jahiz. *Kitab al-bayan wa l-tabyin*. Edited by Muhammad 'Abd al-Salam Harun. 4 vols. 2nd ed. Cairo: Al-Khanji, 1980.

———. *Kitab al-bukhala'*. Edited by Taha al-Hajiri. Cairo: Dar al-Ma'arif, 1971. French translation by Charles Pellat. *Le Livre des avares*. Paris: Maisonneuve et Larosse, 1951. English translation of selections in C. Pellat. *The Life and Works of Jahiz*. Translated by D. M. Hawke. London: Routledge, 1969.

———. "Kitab fasl ma bayn al-'adawa wa l-hasad." In *Rasa'il al-Jahiz*, edited by Muhammad 'Abd al-Salam Harun. 4 vols. Cairo: Al-Khanji, 1964.

———. *Kitab al-hayawan*. Edited by 'Abd al-Salam Harun. 7 vols. Cairo: Al-Babi al-Halabi, 1938–1945.

———. *Kitab al-taj*. French translation by Charles Pellat. *Livre de la couronne*. Paris: Les Belles Lettres, 1954.

126   *References*

—. "Al-ma'ash wa l-ma'ad." In *Rasa'il al-Jahiz*, edited by Muhammad 'Abd al-Salam Harun. 4 vols. Cairo: Al-Khanji, 1964.

—. *Quatre essais*. Translated by Charles Vial. Cairo: Institut français d'archéologie orientale, 1976.

—. *Rasa'il al-Jahiz*, edited by Muhammad 'Abd al-Salam Harun. 4 vols. Cairo: Al-Khanji, 1964.

—. "Risala fi l-hazl wa l-jidd." In *Rasa'il al-Jahiz*, edited by Muhammad 'Abd al-Salam Harun. 4 vols. Cairo: Al-Khanji, 1964.

Al-Jumahi. *Tabaqat fuhul al-shu'ara'*. Edited by Mahmud Muhammad Shakir. 2 vols. Cairo: Al-Madani, 1974.

Al-Jurjani. *Asrar al-balagha*. Edited by Muhammad Rashid Rida. 6th ed. Cairo: Dar al-Manar, 1959.

—. *Dala'il al-i'jaz*. Edited by 'Abd al-Mun'im Khafaja. Cairo: Maktabat al-Qahira, 1969.

Ibn al-Jawzi. *Kitab al-mawdu'at*. Edited by 'Abd al-Rahman Muhammad 'Uthman. 3 vols. Medina: Al-Salafiya, 1966.

—. *Al-Muntazam fi ta'rikh al-muluk wa l-umam*. 6 vols. Hayderabad: Da'irat al-Ma'arif al-'Uthmaniya, 1357–1359 [1938–1940].

Ibn Kathir. *Al-Bidaya wa l-nihaya*. 14 vols. Cairo: Al-Sa'ada, 1932.

Ibn Khallikan. *Wafayat al-a'yan*. Edited by Ihsan 'Abbas. 8 vols. Beirut: Dar Sadir, 1971.

Ibn Manzur. *Akhbar Abi Nuwas*. Cairo: Al-Itimad, 1924.

Ibn Qutayba. *Kitab al-shi'r wa l-shu'ara'*. 2 vols. Beirut: Dar al-thaqafa, 1964.

—. *Ta'wil mukhtalif al-Hadith*. Translated by G. Lecomte. *Le Traité des divergences du "hadith."* Damascus: Institut français de Damas, 1962.

Ibn Rashiq. *Al-'Umda*. Edited by Muhammad Muhyi al-Din 'Abd al-Hamid. 2 vols. Cairo: Al-Hijazi, 1934.

Ibn Tabataba. *'Iyar al-shi'r*. Edited by Taha al-Hajiri and Muhammad Zaghlul Salam. Cairo: Al-Tijariya al-Kubra, 1956.

Plato. *The Republic*. Translated by Paul Shorey. Cambridge: Harvard Univ. Press, 1946.

Al-Qazwini. *Al-Idah fi ʿulum al-balagha*. 4th ed. Beirut: Dar al-Kitab al-Lubnani, 1979.

Qudama b. Jaʿfar. *Naqd al-Shiʿr*. Edited by Kamal Mustafa. Cairo: Al-Khanji, 1963.

Quintilian. *The Institutio oratoria of Quintilian*. Translated by H. E. Butler. Cambridge: Harvard Univ. Press, 1922.

Al-Zawzani. *Sharh al-muʿallaqat al-ʿashr*. Beirut: Dar Maktabat al-Hayah, 1979.

Modern Works

Arberry, A. J. *The Seven Odes: The First Chapter in Arabic Literature*. London: Unwin and Allen, 1957.

Arkoun, M. *Contribution à l'étude de l'humanisme arabe au IVᵉ/Xᵉ siècle*. Paris: Vrin, 1970.

ʿAtr, Nur al-Din. *Manhaj al-naqd fi ʿulum al-Hadith*. 3rd ed. Damascus, 1981.

Barthes, R. "Analyse textuel d'un conte d'Edgar Poe." In *Sémiotique narrative et textuel,* edited by C. Chabrol. Paris: Larousse, 1973.

———. *S/Z*. Paris: Éditions du Seuil, 1970.

———. *S/Z*. Translated by Richard Miller. New York: Hill and Wang, 1974.

Benveniste, E. "Structure des relations de personne dans le verbe." In *Problèmes de linguistique générale*. Paris: Gallimard, 1966.

Berque, J. *Les Dix Grandes Odes arabes de l'Anté-Islam*. Paris: Sindibad, 1979.

Blachère, R. *Histoire de la littérature arabe*. 3 vols. Paris: Adrien-Maisonneuve, 1952.

Bloom, H. *The Anxiety of Influence*. New York: Oxford Univ. Press, 1973.

Borges, Jorge Luis. "Tlön, Uqbar, Orbis Tertius." In *Ficciones,* edited by Anthony Kerrigan, translated by Alastair Reid. New York: Grove Press, 1962.

Compagnon, A. *La Seconde Main*. Paris: Éditions du Seuil, 1979.

128   *References*

Dupont-Roc, R. "Mimesis et énonciation." In *Ecriture et Théorie poétiques.* Paris: Presses de l'École normale supérieure, 1976.

Fontanier, P. *Les Figures du discours.* Paris: Flammarion, 1968.

Fück, J. *ʿArabiya.* Translated by C. Denizeau. Paris: Didier, 1955.

Genette, G. *Figures II.* Paris: Éditions du Seuil, 1969.

———. *Palimpsestes.* Paris: Éditions du Seuil, 1987.

Goldziher, I. *Muslim Studies.* Edited by S. M. Stern, translated by C. R. Barber and S. M. Stern. 2 vols. London: Unwin and Allen, 1967.

Grütter, I. "Arabische Bestattungsbraüche in frühislamischer Zeit." *Der Islam* 31 (1954).

Heinrichs, W. *Arabische Dictung und griechische Poetik.* Beirut, 1969.

Huart, C. "Les séances d'Ibn Naqiya." *Journal asiatique,* 10th ser., 12 (1908).

Husayn, Taha. *Fi l-adab al-jahili.* Cairo, 1927.

———. *Hadith al-arbiʿa.* 10th ed. Cairo: Dar al-maʿarif, n.d.

Juynboll, G. H. A. *Muslim Tradition: Studies in Chronology, Provenance, and Authorship of Early Hadith.* Cambridge: Harvard Univ. Press, 1983.

Khatibi, A., and M. Sijelmassi. *L'Art calligraphique arabe.* Paris: du Chêne, 1976.

Lallot, J. "La Mimesis selon Aristote et l'excellence d'Homère." In *Ecriture et Théorie poétiques.* Paris: Presses de l'École normale supérieure, 1976.

Lejeune, P. *On Autobiography.* Translated by Katherine Leary. Edited by Paul John Eakin. Minneapolis: Univ. of Minnesota Press, 1989.

———. *Le Pacte autobiographique.* Paris: Éditions du Seuil, 1982.

Likhatchev, D. "L'Étiquette littéraire." *Poétique* 9 (1972).

Lombard, M. *Les Textiles dans le monde musulman.* Paris, The Hague, and New York: Mouton, 1978.

Lotman, J. M., and A. Pjatigorskij. "Le Texte et la fonction." *Semiotica* 2 (1982).

Pellat, C. *Le Milieu basrien et la formation de Djâhiz.* Paris: Adrien-Maisonneuve, 1953.

Perec, G. *La Disparition.* Paris: Denoel, 1969.

————. *A Void.* Translated by Gilbert Adair. London: Harvill, 1994.

Peter, H. *Wahrheit und Kunst, Geschichtsschreibung und Plagiat im klassichen Altertum.* Leipzig-Berlin, 1911.

Al-Sandubi, Hasan. *Adab al-Jahiz.* Cairo, 1931.

Schmidt, J.-J. *Les "Mou'allaqat," poésie arabe préislamique.* Paris: Seghers, 1978.

Sells, Michael. *Desert Tracings: Six Classic Arabian Odes.* Middletown, Conn.: Wesleyan Univ. Press, 1989.

Sperber, D. *Le Savoir des anthropologues.* Paris: Hermann, 1982.

Stemplinger, E. *Das Plagiat in der griecheschen Literatur.* Leipzig-Berlin, 1912.

Thurber, James. *The Wonderful O.* New York: Simon and Schuster, 1957.

Todorov, T. *The Conquest of America.* Translated by Richard Howard. New York: Harper and Row, 1994.

————. *La Conquète de l'Amérique.* Paris: Éditions du Seuil, 1982.

————. *Les Genres du discours.* Paris: Éditions du Seuil, 1978.

————. *Genres in Discourse.* Translated by Catherine Porter. Cambridge: Harvard Univ. Press, 1990.

————. *Symbolism and Interpretation.* Translated by Catherine Porter. Ithaca: Cornell Univ. Press, 1982.

————. *Symbolisme et interprétation.* Paris: Éditions du Seuil, 1978.

Tomachevski, B. "Thématique." In *Théorie de la littérature, textes des formalistes russes.* Paris: Éditions du Seuil, 1966.

Trabulsi, A. *La Critique poétique des Arabes jusqu'au Ve siècle de l'hégire.* Damascus, 1955.

Van Ess, J. "L'Autorité de la tradition prophétique dans la théologie mu'tazilite." In *La Notion d'autorité au Moyen Age,* edited by G. Makdisi. Paris: PUF, 1982.

Von Grunebaum, G. E. *Kritik und Dichtkunst.* Wiesbaden, 1955.

Zumthor, P. *Essai de poétique médiévale.* Paris: Éditions du Seuil, 1972.